Daniel Bacon is a solicitor at Duncan Lewis Solicitors in the City of London who specialises in housing law. He regularly acts as Court Duty adviser defending tenants on the possession lists. He also acts for landlords on a private basis. He holds a Master of Laws (LLM) from the University of Law.

Court Duty:

A Reference Guide to Defending Tenants in the Possession Lists

Court Duty:

A Reference Guide to Defending Tenants in the Possession Lists

GENERAL DEFENCES

SECTION 21 DEFENCES

SECTION 8 (THE RENT ARREARS GROUNDS) DEFENCES

Daniel Bacon LLM

Law Brief Publishing

Published 2023 by Law Brief Publishing, an imprint of Law Brief Publishing Ltd
30 The Parks
Minehead
Somerset
TA24 8BT

www.lawbriefpublishing.com

Paperback: 978-1-914608-49-0

PREFACE

I have written this guide primarily as an aide de memoir for myself. And if I find it useful, I hope that others will too.

I am a solicitor charged with attending to the possession lists at Willesden County Court in North-West London. The possession lists are the frontlines of landlord and tenant law, hard-fought trenches where duty solicitors, bent double and knock-kneed, work to represent a steady and sometimes overwhelming flow of unrepresented tenants as a last line of defence against imminent eviction. If we do not succeed, possession in 14 days is the usual order.

The easier it is for a Duty Solicitor to refer to the relevant law and the possible defences to a claim, the better he or she will be able to represent his or her clients and to assist the court. In the following guide I have tried to set out everything I need to have at my fingertips, in a way that I find easy to use. Not just the possible defences and the authorities for the same, but key quotations from said authorities, and authorities as to the discretion of the courts to deal with certain matters in certain ways. This will enable you not only rapidly to find and substantiate defences but will also enable you to assist the court in matters of law, discretion and procedure. This is essential – you may find yourself up against a claimant who is a litigant in person, or a claimant who is represented by a barrister considerably more experienced than you; and you may be before a sitting judge who is very experienced in housing law, or one who is not and who will really benefit from your support. In each of these scenarios, your duty to the court and simultaneously your duty to your client will rarely have a sharper or more urgent focus than on the possession lists.

That is why I have written this guide. To help you to help both the court and the client. And because when in the trenches, it is better to avoid that even more ancient Lie: Dulce et decorum est pro *justitia* mori. I hope that this guide will help you to keep fighting for justice for yet another day.

My sincere thanks must go to a number of parties, not least to Tim and Garry at Law Brief Publishing. They have been a great strength in bringing this book to publication and have consistently supported me with enthusiasm and confidence. I also wish to thank my good friend and colleague William Flack from whom I have learned so much and with whom I occasionally blog and podcast on housing law: thank you. To my colleagues at Duncan Lewis Solicitors and in particular my director Manjinder Atwal who has introduced me to the court duty scheme and has steadfastly shown me the utmost support and guidance and belief: thank you. To the clerks, security, and judges at Willesden County Court with whom I work and who carry out their duties with commitment, equanimity, equity, and good cheer: thank you. To my family, Iva, Freddie and my mother, without whom this and every other endeavour could not possibly have hoped to have been completed: thank you. And to our friend, Dr Timothy Short, for all your help and assistance: thank you. And it would be remiss of me not to thank those who are reading this guide, for all the work you do on court duty or otherwise in housing law, and for ensuring justice can be accessed by all: thank you.

My gratitude and acknowledgment must also go to the very dedicated people who create and maintain some invaluable resources online and in print: in particular, to the legal team at Shelter, to Giles Peaker at Nearly Legal, to HHJ Luba KC, and to Simon Mullings.

The law set out in this guide is believed to be correct and up-to-date as at 12 February 2023.

Daniel Bacon LLM
Solicitor
February 2023

CONTENTS

CHAPTER ONE

GENERAL DISCRETION OF THE COURT AND POSSIBLE ORDERS

In general, a court of first instance dealing with a possession list may, for any claim:

1. Decide the claim (CPR r. 55.8(1)(a))

    - Meaning:

        - Make an order in favour of the claimant, or

        - Dismiss the claim

2. Make directions (CPR r. 55.8(1)(b))

    - If the claim is disputed "on grounds which appear to be substantial", the court must:

        - Make directions including the allocation to either the fast track or the multitrack, or

        - Re-list it for a hearing to enable it to be so allocated (such a directions hearing will usually be given a time estimate of 30 minutes) (CPR r. 55.8(2)).

    - However, the appearance of a defence on grounds which appear to be substantial "is not a precondition to the giving of case management directions under r. 55.8(1)(b)" (Lord Justice Lewison, Birmingham City Council v Stephenson, Court of Appeal (2016)). If there is any discussion about a defence which may be in any way arguable, then the court should be asked to make directions or adjourn to allow directions to be made. If the court is satisfied that the issues being discussed are not in any way arguable then the court may decide the claim as above.

3. Adjourn for a fixed period (CPR r. 3.1(2)(b))

   - This should only be done if it would be in accordance with the overriding objective (CPR r. 1.1)

   - A claim may be adjourned to benefit either the claimant or the defendant, for example, to give a claimant an opportunity to amend a claim, or if possession is sought on discretionary rent arrears grounds and the defendant needs time to resolve a benefit issue. For mortgage possession claims there are separate rules regarding this. A matter should NOT be adjourned for a fixed period to assist a Defendant if a mandatory ground is made out because in such a case the court has NO DISCRETION (Castle Vale Housing Action Trust v Gallagher, Court of Appeal (2001)), even if, in a Ground 8 case, the arrears have only been caused by a problem with benefit payments which is on the verge of being resolved (Marath v MacGillivray, Court of Appeal (1996)).

   - For possession claims sought on discretionary grounds, the court may adjourn for any period that the court deems reasonable.

4. Where possession is sought on discretionary grounds, the court has an inherent jurisdiction to adjourn the claim generally and may do so on terms (s9(1) and (3) Housing Act 1988, and CPR rr. 3.1(2)(b) and 3.1(3)). This does not apply where a mandatory ground is made out (s9(6) Housing Act 1988).

As often as possible, the duty adviser should aim to have the court dismiss a claim, or to adjourn it generally without terms.

In general the court has the following options available, in increasing order of desirability for the defendant:

- Outright possession order
- Possession order suspended on terms
- = Adjournment for a fixed period
- = Directions for a Defence
- Adjournment generally on terms with liberty to restore
- Adjournment generally with liberty to restore
- Claim dismissed

I have mentioned above that the court has no discretion to adjourn (whether for a fixed period or generally, on terms or not) in cases where a mandatory ground is made out, and it is also true that in such cases the court cannot make a possession order suspended on terms – the only option is an outright possession order (see chapter on Exceptional Hardship) (or of course to make directions for a Defence to be filed, or to dismiss the claim).

CHAPTER TWO

SECURITY OF TENURE

Security of tenure is essentially a measure of how difficult it is for a landlord to end a tenancy. Excluded licences (such as those granted to homeless applicants pursuant to Section 188 of the Housing Act 1996, or your typical "lodger" arrangement), for example, do not have any security of tenure and can be ended on reasonable notice and without a court order. Their only "security" is provided by the Protection from Eviction Act and any contractual considerations. This is not security of tenure.

Security of tenure is an allowance under a statutory regime which makes a tenancy agreement not just a matter of contract law, but something more than contract (though the law of contracts still applies to the agreement). It can manifest in ways that are substantive (this is the real, meaty security of tenure), or in ways that are merely procedural. But even a tenancy agreement that has only procedural security of tenure is not just an agreement under contract law – it is something more, and there is more stability for the tenant's tenure than as simply provided by the contract itself.

Assured tenancies gain their security of tenure from the statutory regime of the Housing Act 1988. This guide deals with assured tenancies only – Section 8 and 21 notices are relevant to the statutory regime of the Housing Act 1988 only. Secure tenancies are a different beast and exist under the statutory regime of the Housing Act 1985.

Assured shorthold tenancies have only procedural security of tenure for as long as they are able to rely on Section 21 of the Housing Act 1988. Procedural security of tenure means that the landlord need only to have complied with specific regulations and a specific process to end the tenancy – the tenant need not have done anything wrong at all.

Fully assured tenancies (i.e. non-shorthold) have substantive security of tenure, meaning that they can typically only be ended if the tenant has done something wrong, such as not paying rent. For fully assured tenancies, the landlord will have to demonstrate that one of the grounds in Schedule 2 of the Housing Act 1988 has been met (such as grounds 8, 10 or 11 as dealt with in this guide). For the sake of completeness, secure tenancies also have substantive security of tenure and the grounds for possession are found in Schedule 2 of the Housing Act 1985.

It is worth noting for court duty that in the rarer instances in which you come across a secure tenancy, the relevant notice will be a notice pursuant to Section 83 of the Housing Act 1985. This will look something like a Section 8 notice and will cite grounds in a similar way – but do not be put off because the grounds are different: they are grounds under the 1985 Act, not the 1988 Act.

An assured shorthold tenancy is essentially an assured tenancy to which Section 21 applies. Section 21 provides a no-fault route to eviction. Failures of compliance with regulations can limit or preclude the ability to rely on Section 21 to determine a tenancy, meaning that until such a failure is corrected (if it can be), there is in effect no difference between that tenancy and a fully assured tenancy.

An assured tenancy (whether fully assured or shorthold) will lose its security of tenure under the statutory regime if the tenant no longer lives at the property as his only or principal home. Section 8 and Section 21 will therefore no longer apply.

CHAPTER THREE

REASONABLENESS OF MAKING A POSSESSION ORDER

Some of the grounds in Schedule 2 of the Housing Act 1988 introduce a reasonableness test to the making of a possession order (such as, for grounds 10 and 11). There is no reasonable test for mandatory grounds (such as ground 8), and none for Section 21.

A possession order will be reasonable if it is reasonable in all the circumstances. There is some case law guidance as to what this means in practice, and other suggestions below as to what may be arguable. I do not limit the following table only to the question as it might apply to grounds 10 and 11.

Less reasonable	**Authority**
Notes for Form 3 were not served alongside the notice – the Notes contain considerable information to tenants	Arguable
The notice served was not the correct notice – information to tenants may be missing	Arguable
Rent arrears have only been caused by a benefit issue which is in the process of being resolved.	Arguable
The claimant is a Local Authority or Registered Provider of Social Housing, and they have not adequately followed the Pre-Action Protocol for Possession Claims by Social Landlords.	Arguable

Arrears have accrued but only because the tenant lost his job – he is about to restart work and will be in a position to start paying off the arrears.	Arguable
Arrears have accrued because of medical issues – these are being resolved, and once resolved the tenant will be able to start repaying the arrears.	Arguable
The tenant's breach is not serious, or not repeated, or has been remedied.	Opposite to Bristol City Council v Mousah, Court of Appeal (1997)
Eviction would have particularly adverse consequences for this tenant as it is clear that he will not qualify for Local Authority rehousing on making a homelessness application	London Borough of Lewisham v Adeyemi, Court of Appeal (1999)

More reasonable	**Authority**
The arrears are very high	Arguable
There is no good reason for the arrears	Arguable
Possession for a long-term insistence on breaching the tenancy agreement	Sheffield City Council v Green, Court of Appeal (1993)
Possession for long-term anti-social behaviour towards neighbours (whether a breach of the tenancy agreement or simply falling under Ground 14) by the tenant's child / family member	Royal Borough of Kensington & Chelsea v Simmonds, Court of Appeal (1996)
A "most serious breach" [of the tenancy agreement] – for example, drug dealing at the property	Bristol City Council v Mousah, Court of Appeal (1997)
It is clear that the defendant would be rehoused by the Local Authority on making a homelessness application	London Borough of Lewisham v Adeyemi, Court of Appeal (1999)

Nota Bene – If it is unclear whether or not the defendant would be rehoused after making a homelessness application then this question should not feature at all in the "reasonableness" test (Bristol City Council v Mousah, Court of Appeal (1997)) (London Borough of Lewisham v Adeyemi, Court of Appeal (1999)).

Sheffield City Council v Green, Court of Appeal (1993)

"The tenancy agreement provided in plain terms that the defendant was not allowed to keep a cat, dog or any other animal in the dwelling... [T]he defendant had for many years kept a dog, despite repeated refusals from the local authority [landlord]... It is only in a very special case that the court could properly refuse to give a landlord possession of a tenant who broke a covenant and had insisted on breaking it.

"[However, in this case, the defendant's neighbours wanted to provide witness statements that the dog was "harmless and a friend", but the defendant only raised this on appeal]... If the judge [at first instance] had had all the testimonials supplied and the witnesses had turned up as necessary to explain that the dog was harmless and a friend... it might have had some effect on the judge".

Royal Borough of Kensington & Chelsea v Simmonds, Court of Appeal (1996)

LORD JUSTICE SIMON BROWN: "[There is] no authority for the proposition that the tenant who has tried and failed to control his or her child is immune from a possession order... As to the justice of the position, it must be remembered that not only are the interests of the tenant and her family here at stake; so too are the interests of their neighbours. It would in my judgment be quite intolerable if they were to be held necessarily deprived of all possibility of relief in these cases, merely because some ineffectual tenant next door was incapable of controlling his or her household" [suspended possession order upheld].

Bristol City Council v Mousah, Court of Appeal (1997)

LORD JUSTICE BELDAM: "This was a case where there had been a most serious offence [drug dealing] committed over a period of three or four months at these premises [contrary to an express provision of the tenancy]… Where there is such a serious breach of a condition of the tenancy, it is only in exceptional cases that it could be said that it was not reasonable to make the order [for possession]" [Court of Appeal took the unusual step of substituting its own position on "reasonableness"].

[The court should not get too involved with the possible outcome of a homelessness application:] LORD JUSTICE BELDAM: "Evidence had been given by the appropriate housing officer that, if the respondent applied, his application would be dealt with on its merits. That, in my view, was all that the judge could properly take into account".

London Borough of Lewisham v Adeyemi, Court of Appeal (1999)

LORD JUSTICE SEDLEY: "I am content to accept that if the case is at one of the two poles that I have described (that is to say cases in which an application for rehousing as homeless will manifestly succeed or not succeed) then there is no reason why the judge should not take that fact, because fact it will be, into account as part of the balance of factors by which he assesses the reasonableness of the possession order. But if all the evidence shows is that there would be, on a fresh application, an issue for the local authority to decide, then this court has no power to make a pre-emptive or prefigurative decision for the purpose of gauging whether it is reasonable for it to make a possession order".

CHAPTER FOUR

DEEMED DATE OF SERVICE OF THE NOSP

If the claimant cannot demonstrate on the balance of probabilities a date of actual service of a NOSP it will be extremely important for him to be able to rely on a deemed service provision. The point of deemed service of course is that the claimant does not need to bother proving that the document was received, only that it was sent. Demonstrating deemed service is always preferable for the landlord to demonstrating actual service.

If the claimant is asserting deemed service, first of all it is essential to establish whether or not the claimant has the right to rely on deemed service, and secondly – if he does have that right – it is essential to calculate the deemed date of service.

Working out the deemed date of service is so important in such circumstances because the notice period given by the NOSP is fundamental to the validity of the proceedings, and the required notice period cannot start until the notice has been served. It is also essential because it is from the date of actual or deemed service that the limitation clock for issuing proceedings will commence. The adviser should always therefore establish the actual or deemed date of service of the NOSP.

It is for the claimant to demonstrate service, and he or she will usually have filed a Certificate of Service in evidence of this. This will of course list the relevant deemed dates of service as per the CPR rules, e.g. 2 business days for first class post. However, the CPR does not apply to NOSPs – it only applies to service in court proceedings, and NOSPs by their very nature are not "in" proceedings. The claimant therefore cannot use the CPR rules to determine a deemed date of service for a NOSP. It may be therefore that the date of service given in the Particulars of Claim is not, on closer inspection, accurate, so do not rely on it.

There should, in a well-drafted tenancy agreement, be a deemed service provision. This may take the form of simply incorporating Section 196 of the Law of Property Act 1925, or it may be an express clause specific to that agreement. It is often argued that without being incorporated into the tenancy agreement expressly, Section 196 of the Law of Property Act 1925 does not automatically apply to NOSPs, using the authority of Wandsworth Borough Council v Atwell, Court of Appeal (1995). However, it seems to me that this may not be quite the full story, and it seems to me that this case may in fact be authority for the proposition that if the tenancy agreement does not expressly require service of a NOSP to determine the tenancy then s196 does not automatically apply and it (or another deemed service provision) would have to be incorporated to be relied on.

If the tenancy agreement incorporates (or otherwise can rely on, as above) s196 of the Law of Property Act 1925 and the method used is one of the methods permitted by that section (i.e. (i) affixing the notice or leaving it for the tenant on the land or any house or building comprised in the lease, (ii) leaving the notice at the tenant's last-known place of abode or business in the United Kingdom, or (iii) sending the notice by registered post to the tenant by name and it not being returned undelivered), then it is irrelevant whether or not the tenant received the notice. This is a pure "deemed service" provision. The claimant only needs to demonstrate on the balance of probabilities that s196 is effectively incorporated or can otherwise be effectively relied upon (perhaps difficult to do without express incorporation given the status quo that exists in understanding the authority) and that he used one of the stated methods for service (and in the case of registered post, it was not returned undelivered).

If the tenancy agreement does incorporate Section 196 of the Law of Property Act 1925 then, by extension, Section 7 of the Interpretation Act 1978 will also be incorporated (London Borough of Southwark v Runa Akhtar, Stel LLC, Upper Tribunal (Lands Chamber) (2017)). This extends the methods of service covered by the deemed service provision to service by First Class Post. However, where a landlord seeks to rely on deemed service of a notice by First Class Post as a consequence of Section 7, it *is* relevant whether or not the tenant actually received the notice as this is only a partial deemed service provision. Section 7 creates a presumption of service once the claimant has demonstrated on the balance of probabilities that he properly addressed, pre-paid and posted the notice, but this presumption is rebuttable. The burden of proof then shifts to the tenant to PROVE on the balance of probabilities that he did not in fact receive the notice. A bare denial however, even under oath, is insufficient to rebut the presumption (London Borough of Southwark v Runa Akhtar, Stel LLC, Upper Tribunal (Lands Chamber) (2017)). If the tenant can however rebut this presumption on the balance of probabilities then service will not have been effected, and the landlord will have to demonstrate actual service.

If the tenancy agreement has an express deemed service provision (i.e. not just an incorporation, but specifically setting out the rules in black and white in the agreement itself), stipulating that a notice will be deemed served after a specified period of time, and the method used was in line with that provision, then again it is irrelevant whether or not the tenant received the notice. The claimant only needs to demonstrate on the balance of probabilities that the clause exists, is valid, and the method used was the method stipulated, and this will be a pure deemed service provision.

When calculating a date of deemed service (once you are satisfied that any such date can be relied on) then it is important not to rely on the CPR rules as these do not apply. If there is an express provision in the tenancy agreement, then this must give the method of calculating the timeframe within which service will be deemed by any permissible method. Where Section 196 is incorporated (or can otherwise be relied on), and either Section 196 or Section 7 is relied upon, then the appropriate calculation is (as it seems to me) set out in the table below. You may face some resistance to the following calculations because of the familiarity of the CPR rules, but in my view the following must be the correct calculations by virtue of the wording of the legislation. The legislation uses the phrase “in the ordinary course of post”, and where else to look for that than the official Royal Mail delivery estimates? The

CPR is not designed to give deemed service in line with "the ordinary course of post" (consider, for example, the fact that a postal method that gives next day delivery provides for deemed served after 2 days – and the Criminal Procedure Rules are even longer!) so in my view it is not a relevant yardstick for these purposes.

Method of service	Deemed date of service	Authority for the deemed date of service
First class post	Next day	Royal Mail delivery estimate. S7 Interpretation Act 1978.
Second class post	3 days	Royal Mail delivery estimate. S7 Interpretation Act 1978.
Email	Immediate	Sch. 1 Interpretation Act 1978.
Personal service	Immediate	N/A
Registered post	Next day	Royal Mail delivery estimate. S196(4) Law of Property Act 1925.
Left at last known place of residence	Immediate	S196(3) Law of Property Act 1925.

If no provision for deemed service can be relied upon then the claimant will have to rely on old common law rules for actual service. These are complex and are dealt with in the relevant chapter in this guide, but essentially the claimant will have to prove to the civil standard that the notice was brought to the tenant's attention. This can be difficult to prove, but generally will require personal service and the instruction of a process server and a Witness Statement in evidence.

Authority that CPR deemed service provisions do not apply to NOSPs

1. The CPR applies to "all proceedings in (a) the County Court; (b) the High Court; and (c) the Civil Division of the Court of Appeal" (CPR r. 2.1(1));

2. Proceedings may not be begun until after the expiry of the NOSP (see the chapter on limitation for more authority on this);
3. Therefore the NOSP is not "in" proceedings;
4. Therefore CPR rules for deemed service do not apply to NOSPs.

Authority that s196 LPA 1925 does not automatically apply to NOSPs without express incorporation into the tenancy agreement or an express requirement for service of a NOSP to determine the tenancy

- s196 LPA 1925 automatically applies to all notices "required" to be served by any instrument, and while a tenancy agreement is an instrument, if it does not make an express provision requiring the service of a notice to quit to determine the tenancy then it does not "require" the service of a NOSP (i.e. it is not enough that the requirement for a NOSP is implied at common law or imported by statute). In such a case, s196 cannot be relied upon (Wandsworth Borough Council v Atwell, Court of Appeal (1995)).

What types of deemed service can be relied on?

Provision	Basis of Authority	Method of service allowed	When is service deemed?	Can service be disputed?
S196 Law of Property Act 1925	Must be expressly incorporated into the tenancy agreement (Wandsworth Borough Council v Atwell, Court of Appeal (1995)).	affixing to the house / leaving on the land (s196(3) Law of Property Act 1925).	Immediate (s196(3) Law of Property Act 1925).	No.
		Leaving at last known place of abode or business (s196(3) Law of Property Act 1925).	Immediate (s196(3) Law of Property Act 1925).	No.
		Sending it by registered post, this not being returned as undelivered (s196(4) Law of Property Act 1925).	"at the time at which the registered letter would in the ordinary course be delivered" (s196(4) Law of Property Act 1925).	No.
S7 Interpretation Act 1978	If s196 is expressly incorporated into the tenancy agreement then s7 can be automatically relied upon (London Borough of Southwark v Runa Akhtar, Stel LLC, Upper Tribunal (2017)).	Post (any class) – "properly addressing, pre-paying and posting" (s7 Interpretation Act 1978).	"at the time at which the letter would be delivered in the ordinary course of post" (s7 Interpretation Act 1978).	Yes – if Defendant can prove he did not receive it (s7 Interpretation Act 1978). A bare denial, even under oath, is insufficient (London Borough of Southwark v Runa Akhtar, Stel LLC, Upper Tribunal (Lands Chamber) (2017)).
Specific express provision	Specific provision in the tenancy agreement, must state method(s) of service allowed, and after how long the notice etc. will be deemed served.	As per the tenancy agreement.	As per the tenancy agreement.	As per the tenancy agreement.

Section 7 Interpretation Act 1978

Where an Act authorises or requires any document to be served by post… then… the service is deemed to be effected by properly addressing, pre-paying and posting a letter containing the document and… to have been effected at the time at which the letter would be delivered in the ordinary course of post.

Sch. 1 Interpretation Act 1978

"Writing" includes typing… and other modes of representing or reproducing words in a visible form, and expressions referring to writing are construed accordingly.

Section 196 Law of Property Act 1925

…

(3) Any notice required or authorised by this Act to be served shall be sufficiently served if it is left at the last-known place of abode or business in the United Kingdom of the lessee… or… is affixed or left for him on the land or any house or building comprised in the lease…

(4) Any notice required or authorised by this Act to be served shall also be sufficiently served, if it is sent by post in a registered letter addressed to the lessee… by name, at the aforesaid place of abode or business… and if that letter is not returned… undelivered; and that service shall be deemed to be made at the time at which the registered letter would in the ordinary course be delivered.

London Borough of Southwark v Runa Akhtar, Stel LLC, Upper Tribunal (Lands Chamber) (2017)

HHJ ELIZABETH COOKE (sitting as a Deputy Judge of the Upper Tribunal): "The Appellant's argument [sets out] as follows:

a. Section 196 permits the service by registered post or recorded delivery… or by "any other instrument";

b. Section 196 therefore authorises the service of certain documents by post;

c. Therefore wherever Section 196 applies, Section 7 of the Interpretation Act 1978 also applies.

"In Chiswell Estates v Griffon Land (1975) the Court of Appeal proceeded on this this basis, without discussion but without any suggestion that the point was in doubt... It seems to me that the Appellant's reasoning is sound...

"Accordingly I find that because s196 applies to the [notice], so does s7 of the Interpretation Act 1978.

[Regarding rebuttal of the Section 7 presumption]:

HHJ ELIZABETH COOKE: "A legal presumption like the one in Section 7 has the effect of reversing the burden of proof. Once the landlord has proved that the notice was properly addressed, pre-paid and posted it has nothing further to do – unless the contrary is proved. If the contrary is proved, then the landlord must, as it were, go the long way round and actually prove service without the help of the presumption, and must therefore convince the tribunal on the balance of probabilities that the notice was actually received. But it is only required to do that if the contrary is proved, and not if the contrary is merely asserted.

"Ms Akhtar's evidence went no further than a bare denial. The absence of the notice in her filing system adds nothing. The evidence about her lodger was not evidence that the notices had not been delivered, but was merely the ruling out of an explanation for her not having seen them. As a matter of law, what Ms Akhtar said was not sufficient to rebut the presumption in Section 7 of the Interpretation Ant 1978. That is the case even if the FTT was convinced that Ms Akhtar was not telling lies, because memories can fail, envelopes can be mislaid, items of post can be overlooked".

Wandsworth Borough Council v Atwell, Court of Appeal (1995)

LORD JUSTICE GLIDWELL: "In my judgment a tenancy agreement which makes no express provision for the service of a notice to quit to determine the tenancy does not "require" such a notice to be served. Thus in that situation section 196(5) does not apply… The moral for landlords is clear. If they wish to render valid and effective service [by deemed service] without proving it came to the attention of the lessee, they must: (i) make express provision for such a method of service in the tenancy agreement; and (ii) prove the terms of the agreement in any action for possession following service of such a notice".

LORD JUSTICE WAITE: "The use [in section 196(5) of the Law of Property Act 1925] of the phrase "notices required to be served by any instrument" provides a plain indication that the subsection is only to apply in cases where the requirement of service is one that appears explicitly on the face of the instrument. Those words would not be apt to describe a case where the requirement of service is merely implied at common law, or is imported by statute".

CHAPTER FIVE

ACTUAL SERVICE OF THE NOSP

If the claimant cannot rely on a deemed service provision, then he will have to prove to the court actual service to the civil standard. Actual service occurs when a notice is brought to the attention of the recipient. This may (most clearly) be achieved by personal service on the individual recipient, and the rules for this are set out in the following chapter. However, the common law has over hundreds of years developed rules setting out some parameters for demonstrating that actual service has been achieved to the civil standard without recourse to direct personal service in every instance.

Lady Hale gives a summary of the position on actual-service-other-than-personal service at paragraph 14 of her Supreme Court judgment in Haywood v Newcastle-upon-Tyne Hospitals NHS Foundation Trust (2018). Citing authorities back to Jones on the demise of Griffiths v Marsh in 1791, she concluded that the common law allows actual service of a notice "upon an agent authorised to accept it".

It was held in Haywood v Newcastle-upon-Tyne Hospitals NHS Foundation Trust, Supreme Court (2018) in a majority view that there is no common law deemed service provision covering service by post. The common law deals only with actual service – which includes service upon an agent.

Actual service can be demonstrated at common law therefore (for example) by any of the following methods. If it can be demonstrated to the civil standard that any of the following methods were used, then this will adequately raise a presumption to the civil standard that the notice has been brought to the attention of the tenant.

Method	**Authority**
Personal service	See the following chapter
Delivering the notice to the tenant's servant… … but only if it is explained to the servant that it is an eviction notice… … and only if the servant is expressly directed at the time of delivery to give the notice to the tenant himself.	Jones d Griffiths v Marsh (1791), Doe d Neville v Dunbar (1826), Papillon v Brunton (1860) Doe dem Buross v Lucas (1804) Smith v Clark (1840)
Delivering the notice to the tenant's adult children at the property… … but only if it is explained to the tenant's adult child that it is an eviction notice… … and only if the tenant's adult child is expressly directed at the time of delivery to give the notice to the tenant himself.	Tanham v Nicholson (1872) Doe dem Buross v Lucas (1804) Smith v Clark (1840)
Delivering the notice to the tenant's wife… … but only if it is explained to the tenant's wife that it is an eviction notice… … and only if the tenant's wife is expressly directed at the time of delivery to give the notice to the tenant himself.	Doe dem Buross v Lucas (1804) Doe dem Buross v Lucas (1804) Smith v Clark (1840)

CHAPTER SIX

PERSONAL SERVICE OF THE NOSP

For the reasons given in the chapter on deemed service, the CPR does not apply to NOSPs.

Courts should find the CPR rules (and their common law interpretation) on personal service very persuasive however. The courts have drawn extensively on pre-CPR common law rules when trying to understand the legal principles for CPR-compliant personal service. Therefore, although the *CPR provisions* below do not themselves apply to personal service of NOSPs, the common law rules should set out the position when establishing personal service – whether under the CPR or not.

Personal service is "when the notice actually reaches the recipient's hands" (Lady Black in Haywood v Newcastle-upon-Tyne Hospitals Foundation Trust, Supreme Court (2018)).

- The House of Lords in Kenneth Allison Ltd v A.E. Limehouse & Co in 1992 set out a 2-limb test for ascertaining personal service in a pre-CPR context (if either limb is satisfied then personal service has been effected):

  1. The document is handed to the person to be served; or

  2. If he will not accept it, he is told what the document contains and the document is left with or near him.

  LORD BRIDGE OF HARWICH: "There is abundant authority for the proposition that personal service requires that the document be handed to the person to be served or, if he will not accept it, that he be told what the document contains and the document be left with or near him".

- CPR r. 6.5(3)(a) states that personal service is effected on an individual "by leaving it with that individual".

- In the High Court case of Tseitline v Mikhelson (2015) it was common ground that the two-limb common law test above <u>does</u> apply to understanding personal service under the CPR and should be used to ascertain whether personal service is effected under CPR r. 6.5(3)(a). Likewise, it seems correct that the decisions in Tseitline should feed back into the non-CPR strictly common law rules.

- The High Court in Tseitline v Mikhelson (2015) set out the following rules for interpreting the two limbs of the test in Kenneth Allison Ltd v AE Limehouse & Co (1992):

<u>In respect of the First Limb</u>

1. For the "document to be handed" to the person to be served, that person must accept taking it, and the process server must <u>let go of it in the recipient's hand</u> however briefly.

2. For this limb to be satisfied, the "nature" of the documents must be stated clearly on the envelope (etc.) and be "immediately and readily apparent" (no further explanation is required by the process servers under this limb).

<u>In respect of the Second Limb</u>

1. If the person to be served will not accept the document, for it to be "left with or near" him the process server must <u>let go of it and leave it near him</u> such that the recipient has "a sufficient degree of possession of the document to enable him to exercise dominion over it for any period of time however brief". This still applies even if the process server subsequently picks up the document again and takes it away (the recipient having refused to pick it up).

2. If the person to be served will not accept the document, for him to be "told what the document contains" requires it to

be explained to him that it is "a legal document requiring their attention in connection with proceedings". For a NOSP the equivalent is presumably to explain that this is an eviction notice requiring the recipient to give up possession of the property, and that this is the first step prior to the commencement of proceedings, or something to that effect.

3. If the recipient does not speak English, for him to be "told what the document contains" under this limb it is enough if one of his "companions" speaks English and understands the explanation.

4. Knowledge of what the document contains can be inferred from the intended recipient's behaviour.

The burden of demonstrating proper service always lies with the claimant.

CHAPTER SEVEN

RAISING A DEFENCE OF SET OFF AGAINST ARREARS

When a Defendant approaches you with complaints of (for example) disrepair or harassment (I shall henceforth refer only to disrepair for ease of reference) and wishes to defend a claim for possession on grounds of rental arrears, it can sometimes be a difficult business knowing how best to proceed, especially if the arrears are quite high. Will the counterclaim be valuable enough to amount to a Defence? Does the Defendant qualify for Legal Aid or would a CFA be a possibility, or would the Defendant be interested in privately funding a defence and counterclaim (which may become extremely protracted) if he or she had to pay? Does the Defendant have evidence of the matter at hand, such as photographs or reports? With all these aspects in mind, is it best to fight or attempt to settle?

If the court considers any potential defence to be only fanciful they are not obliged to make directions. But in all but the most obvious cases, how can we be sure of the threshold at which a potential defence of set-off is fancifully low-value, and how do we persuade a resistant judge that the disrepair claimed of (etc.) may well be above that threshold? To do so successfully we must do so confidently and with authority.

In the appropriate section of this guide, dealing with Section 8 specific defences, I set out a common methodology for calculating potential damages for disrepair. It is merely rough and ready and is not to be relied upon when calculating exact figures in the cool light of day, but only to give some idea of value in a few minutes on the court duty desk.

There is the possibility of other grounds as well – harassment, unlawful eviction, as well as discrimination, breach of the Public Sector Equality Duty, and others.

It is very important to note that a clause in the tenancy agreement that purports to exclude the tenant's right to a defence of set-off is likely to be an unfair term. Authorities below. Any attempt by the claimant to rely on any such clause should be firmly resisted.

Date of tenancy	**Authority that a clause purporting to exclude the right to a defence of set-off is an unfair term**
Tenancy agreements where the most recent written contract commenced <u>before 1/10/2015</u>	Sch. 2 para. 1(b) Unfair Terms in Consumer Contracts Regulations 1999
Tenancy agreements where the most recent written contract commenced <u>on or after 1/10/2015</u>	Sch. 2 para. 2 Consumer Rights Act 2015

It is also important to note that in calculating your set off against arrears you may apply the Simmons v Castle 10% uplift to all general and tortious damages. You can also ask for interest which falls within the court's general discretion to grant. The judgment debt rate is 8%, but the courts typically apply a "commercial" rate which is considered to be 1% above the base rate. These little extras can all add up and – especially in what may seem a marginal case – may be enough to persuade a reluctant judge to adjourn for a Defence and Counterclaim to be filed.

CHAPTER EIGHT

GAS SAFETY RECORDS AND THE VALIDITY OF A SECTION 21 NOTICE

[It is worth noting that the Gas Safety requirements came into force on 1 October 2015. If the tenancy began before that date and there is no replacement tenancy that commenced on or after that date, then the following rules and restrictions do not apply. This watershed applies equally to service of the EPC and How to Rent Guide. The watershed does not however apply to deposit protection matters].

For some time after the county court judgment of His Honour Judge Luba KC (then QC) in Caridon Property Ltd v Monty Shooltz, Central London County Court (2018), it was held that (1) a failure to serve a Gas Safety certificate that covered the period at the start of the tenancy, and (2) a failure to serve this certificate prior to the start of the tenancy, were both fatal errors to the ability of a landlord to rely on Section 21 to recover possession. Neither of these were errors that could be rectified later on.

The Court of Appeal in Trecarrell House Limited v Patricia Rouncefield (2020) has changed the position on the second of these two issues. Late service of a gas safety certificate <u>does not</u> preclude the subsequent service of a valid Section 21 notice. If the landlord does not serve the gas safety certificate before the start of the tenancy, he can simply serve it later on. However, the first of the two issues remains: The gas safety certificate must cover the start of the tenancy, and if it does not then the landlord is (probably) prevented from serving a valid Section 21 notice forever (in respect of that and any replacement tenancy).

Trecarrell House Limited v Patricia Rouncefield, Court of Appeal (2020) was also clear that any subsequent Gas Safety Records produced must also be served on the tenant at the time of or prior to service of the Section

21 Notice, for the notice to be valid. What is not clear is whether any subsequent GSRs need to be produced at all (only that if they are, they must be served). According to the criminal law, GSRs need to be produced no more than every 12 months, but for Section 21 validity they can be late – perhaps indefinitely late!

It may be worthwhile – if there is no valid GSR produced and served which covers the date of service of the Section 21 notice – to raise this as a defence. The authorities you would have to rely on are hesitant on this point, but you could argue that although Trecarrell is clear that the "once in 12 months" requirement is not strictly relevant for Section 21 validity, nonetheless Trecarrell was clear in its expectation that a subsequent GSR <u>would be provided</u> – even if it was a bit late. To allow a subsequent GSR to be indefinitely late (i.e. to simply not be produced) would make a mockery of the Gas Safety Regulations and cannot be what Parliament intended when it linked Section 21 validity to gas safety. At the very least, this is a defence which appears to be substantial, or is a defence which is arguable and not fanciful, and must lead to directions for a Defence.

You should see the relevant Defences in this guide for more details.

CHAPTER NINE

THE EXCEPTIONAL HARDSHIP TEST

If a possession order is made on mandatory grounds then "the giving up of possession shall not be postponed... to a date later than fourteen days after the making of the order, unless it appears to the court that exceptional hardship would be caused by requiring possession to be given up by that date; and shall not in any event be postponed to a date later than six weeks after the making of the order" (Section 89(1) Housing Act 1980).

This 6-week limit does not apply to mortgage claims or possession on discretionary grounds, and there is therefore no "exceptional hardship" test in such cases (Section 89(2)(a) and (c) Housing Act 1980, respectively).

There is essentially no statutory guidance on what might amount to exceptional hardship in practice. And as this question only arises once a court of first instance has already decided that a requirement for mandatory possession is made out, it is not a point of law that is typically appealed and I am not aware of any such appeals, meaning that there is a dearth of binding case law authority as well.

All I can offer therefore is my view of what works in practice, and my view of the applicable test.

It seems clear to me, and my view is supported by my experience of arguments that have been successful and not successful in this matter, that the test in question is a two-part test:

1. By making a possession order, would the Defendant suffer a hardship that is out-of-the-ordinary, that is, "exceptional"?

2. If yes, could that hardship be alleviated (in part or in whole) by a longer order, up to a maximum of 6 weeks, as compared to a 14-day order?

As to the first part of the test, it is very clear that "exceptional" means out-of-the-ordinary. That is, would this Defendant by being evicted suffer a hardship that is out-of-the-ordinary when compared to the hardships most other people would suffer when being evicted? Needing time to pack, or arrange removals, is not sufficient – everyone facing eviction has to deal with this. Needing time to find a new place to live is not sufficient – everyone facing eviction has to deal with this. Having children in a local school and not wanting to disrupt them in the ordinary course of the school year is not sufficient – everyone with children facing eviction has to deal with this. It has to be something out-of-the-ordinary for the general population or for the relevant group to which this particular Defendant belongs (for example, people with children at a local school).

As to the second part of the test, there are of course academic arguments to be had about the wording of the statute as compared to this, but I do not consider, if the court found that the same exceptional hardship would be caused by a 6-week order as a 14-day order, that they would make a 6-week order. For example, if the exceptional hardship could only possibly be alleviated in 6 months, or 6 years, and 6 weeks would be utterly insufficient, why make a 6-week order? What would be the point? The court, in my view, would be content to make a 14-day order. It is worth noting here that 6 weeks is the maximum the court can go to and it is a limit not a target – the court will generally give the minimum time it considers sufficient to allow the possibility that the exceptional hardship will be alleviated, whether that be a 3 week, 4 week, 5 week, or 6 week order.

My view is that if the issue can be clarified as per the two-part test above then this is how the courts in practice will apply the exceptional hardship threshold. Make no mistake – it is a high threshold, but this approach is a winning one.

Below I set out some examples of court-of-first-instance decisions where a finding was made of exceptional hardship. It is important (or at least preferable) to have evidence of the matters the Defendant raises.

Unreported, Willesden County Court (2022)	D is awaiting an imminent decision on immigration status, and to be evicted prior to receiving this would compromise his ability to make a homelessness application to the Local Authority (in respect of eligibility). 6 weeks is far more likely to be sufficient time than 14 days.
Unreported, Willesden County Court (2022)	D is awaiting major surgery at a local hospital which will not take place within 14 days, but will take place within 6 weeks, and if evicted before the surgery he would risk not being able to keep his preparatory appointments or his actual surgery appointment.
Unreported, Willesden County Court (2022)	A family of 7 children is exceptional and if the family cannot find accommodation because of this then hardship will be caused by a 14-day order which may be alleviated by a longer order (4 weeks in this case).
Unreported, Willesden County Court (2022)	A national holiday period may interfere with an applicant's ability to access homelessness support, so an extension of the possession period may be given to allow for this (e.g. a 3 week order).

CHAPTER TEN

COSTS

It is important to note at the beginning of this section that a costs order is always a discretionary order, and regardless of any contractual clause in the tenancy agreement the court always retains its discretion on costs per CPR r. 44.2(1). (Gomba Holdings UK Ltd v Minories Finance Ltd (No. 2) (1993), Church Commissioners v Ibrahim (1997)).

The fixed costs regime under CPR 45 will apply to undefended Section 8 rent arrears claims, undefended accelerated Section 21 possession claims, and all other Section 21 claims and all other claims for possession whether defended or not, and where it applies should be the starting point for costs decisions (CPR r. 45.1(1)). However, where the tenancy agreement contains a clause explicitly allowing the landlord to recover his costs for obtaining possession, then the starting point for the costs discussion should always be the claimant's schedule of costs (Gomba Holdings UK Ltd v Minories Finance Ltd (No. 2) (1993), Church Commissioners v Ibrahim (1997)).

<u>If the fixed costs regime applies and there is no contractual term to the contrary</u>, the claimant's legal costs recovery should be limited to fixed costs as set out in Table 3 in CPR r. 45.5. In most cases this will amount to £69.50. In addition, for rent arrears claims, there is a fixed judgment fee of £57.25 (where the claim is undefended) (CPR r. 45.6(1)). In addition the claimant will be entitled to the court fee of £355. For the record, and although you will not come across this on court duty, the fixed legal costs recovery in an accelerated Section 21 claim (undefended) is £79.50.

Usual Costs Recovery under the Fixed Fee Regime

Type of Claim	Constituents of the Fixed Costs	Fixed Costs Total
Claims for possession (including s21 claims where arrears are also claimed)	£355 plus £69.50	£424.50
Claims for possession where one of the grounds is rent arrears	£355 plus £69.50 plus £57.25	£481.75
Accelerated claim for possession	£355 plus £79.50	£434.50

If the fixed costs regime applies but there is a contractual term to the contrary, the claimant's costs recovery will rely on the court's discretion in CPR r. 45.1(1) to disapply the fixed costs regime, which discretion the court will be bound to exercise by case law authority (Lord Justice Moore-Bick has commented in Solomon v Cromwell Group PLC (2011) that the fixed costs regime is "subject to any agreement between the parties to the contrary"). The court will then rely on its general discretion on costs under CPR r. 44.2(1), and in exercising this discretion the court will be bound to use as its starting point the claimant's schedule of costs (Gomba Holdings UK Ltd v Minories Finance Ltd (No. 2) (1993), Church Commissioners v Ibrahim (1997)).

If the fixed costs regime does not apply (and therefore does not need to be disapplied) and there is a contractual term regarding costs recovery, the claimant will rely on the court's general discretion on costs under CPR r. 44.3(1) and again the court will be bound to use as its starting point the claimant's schedule of costs (Gomba Holdings UK Ltd v Minories Finance Ltd (No. 2) (1993), Church Commissioners v Ibrahim (1997)).

If the fixed costs regime does not apply and there is no contractual term regarding costs recovery, the court will again determine the matter of costs by exercising its general discretion on costs under CPR r. 44.2(1) and there may be a persuasive argument to be made in this scenario that the court should restrict costs recovery to the levels under the fixed fee regime even though the regime does not strictly-speaking apply, and not to use the claimant's schedule of costs as its starting point, if the only reason that the fixed costs regime does not apply is that the Defendant has raised an (unsuccessful) defence at the first possession hearing at which you are duty. The regime was introduced to ensure that litigation is conducted at proportionate cost as per the overriding objective, but it was surely not introduced to discourage appropriate defences from being tested or questions raised at a first hearing. It is for the court to be satisfied as to the appropriate grounds for possession being made out – the Defendant cannot "consent" to a possession order and if question marks that could be dealt with by the court at a first hearing are not raised for fear of costs consequences then not only are the parties failing to assist the court in its determination but any possession order made in such circumstances may be subject to further litigation if the Defendant were to take subsequent legal advice. If the question marks have been raised and dealt with at the first hearing then the claimant has not suffered any additional costs in any event. The court should be asked respectfully to award costs in line with what would have been recoverable under the fixed costs regime only.

Many ASTs have clauses allowing the landlord to recover costs, although such clauses are written in a wide variety of ways and should always be checked. If a claimant wants their costs, they should always be put to proof to cite the clause in the tenancy agreement that allows them to have their costs awarded. Although the courts have confirmed the primacy of these contractual terms, any costs awarded will still be subject to a reasonableness test and so the Claimant's schedule of costs should always be scrutinised if it is going to apply. Except in the most complex cases, Grade A and B fee earners should not perform more than a supervisory role.

The claimant may cite a clause for costs which on closer inspection does not deal with this matter adequately. It needs to be clearly an agreement that the landlord can recover costs in possession proceedings. There is no magic wording, but it needs to convey this meaning. A clause stating a penalty or setting out administrative fees if rent is late, is not sufficient. The clause may state (an example I have encountered) that the landlord can recover costs for possession where the defendant behaves unreasonably. The claimant argued that it was unreasonable of the defendant not to have vacated at the expiry of the Notice of Seeking Possession. I argued (unsuccessfully in this case, but I think it is still an argument worth raising) that it cannot be considered unreasonable for a tenant to exercise his statutory rights by continuing to occupy a property under an assured shorthold tenancy. The tenancy did not come to an end on the expiry of the Notice of Seeking Possession: the defendant is still an assured shorthold tenant, and it is only the court that can bring the tenancy to an end. It would be unreasonable to expect a tenant to vacate a property prior to the tenancy being brought to an end in the proper manner as by doing so he would be excluding himself from Local Authority homelessness support as such an action would most likely lead to a finding of intentional homelessness under Section 196(1) of the Housing Act 1996. The reasonable course of action for the tenant would be to exercise his statutory rights, to retain occupancy of a property of which he continues to be a tenant, and to continue paying rent, until such time as the tenancy is brought lawfully to an end by the court. This is the course of action the Defendant has taken. The contractual clause relating to costs only applies in the event of the tenant's unreasonable conduct, and it should be submitted that this action does not amount to unreasonable conduct.

If the claimant is citing a contractual clause which you are able to exclude from applicability, then the Defendant will clearly be in a better position for you to argue on his behalf on the matter of costs.

Gomba Holdings (UK) Ltd v Minories Finance Ltd (No. 2), Court of Appeal (1993)

LORD JUSTICE SCOTT: "A clause entitling a mortgagee to recover legal costs from the mortgagor does not extend to costs that were unreasonably incurred or were unreasonable in amount… There is no jurisdictional reason why a [court] should not assess the costs to which a party has become contractually entitled".

Church Commissioners for England v Ibrahim, Court of Appeal (1997)

[The principles set out in Gomba (above) apply to tenancies and leases, not just mortgage cases].

Macleish v Littlestone, Court of Appeal (2016)

LORD JUSTICE BRIGGS: "By virtue of CPR 44.3(1) costs will not be allowed if they were unreasonably incurred or unreasonable in amount… Where the court assesses costs which are payable… under the terms of a contract, CPR 44.5(1) provides… that the costs payable under those terms are, unless the contract expressly provides otherwise, to be presumed to be costs which have been reasonably incurred, and which are reasonable in amount".

Solomon v Cromwell Group PLC, Court of Appeal (2011)

LORD JUSTICE MOORE-BICK: "Subject to any agreement between the parties to the contrary, neither can recover more or less by way of costs than is provided for under the fixed fee regime".

CPR r. 44.2(1)

The court has discretion as to –

(a) whether costs are payable by one party to another;

(b) the amount of those costs; and

(c) when they are to be paid.

CPR r. 45.1(1)

This section sets out the amounts which, unless the court orders otherwise, are to be allowed in respect of legal representatives' charges.

Table 3, CPR r. 45.5

Fixed costs on commencement of a claim for the recovery of land or a demoted claim		
Where the claim form is served by the court or by any method other than personal service by the claimant	Where – • the claim form is served personally by the claimant; and • there is only one defendant	Where there is more than one defendant, for each additional defendant personally served at separate addresses by the claimant
£69.50	£77.00	£15.00

The Starting Point for Costs Assessment at the First Hearing, and the Court's Discretion to Deviate from this

Is there a Contractual clause?	Does the Fixed Costs Regime apply?	Starting point for costs	Authority	Discretion to deviate from the starting point	Authority
None, or can be excluded	Applies	Fixed costs	CPR r. 45.1	None	Solomon v Cromwell Group PLC, Court of Appeal (2011)
	Does not apply	Schedule of costs	CPR r. 44.2(2)(a)	The court's usual discretion In particular as to: Reasonableness of conduct Reasonable in amount Reasonably incurred Proportionate	CPR r. 44.2(2)(b) CPR r. 44.2(4)(a) CPR r. 44.3(1) CPR r. 44.3(1) CPR r. 44.3(2)(a)
Present and cannot be excluded	Applies	Schedule of Costs	Solomon v Cromwell Group PLC, Court of Appeal (2011) Gomba Holdings (UK) Ltd v Minories Finance Ltd (No. 2), Court of Appeal (1993)	The court's usual discretion In particular as to: Reasonableness of conduct Reasonable in amount Reasonably incurred Proportionate	CPR r. 44.2(2)(b) CPR r. 44.2(4)(a) CPR r. 44.3(1) CPR r. 44.3(1) CPR r. 44.3(2)(a) Gomba Holdings (UK) Ltd v Minories Finance Ltd (No. 2), Court of Appeal (1993)
	Does not apply	Schedule of Costs	CPR r. 44.2(2)(a)	The court's usual discretion In particular as to: Reasonableness of conduct Reasonable in amount Reasonably incurred Proportionate	CPR r. 44.2(2)(b) CPR r. 44.2(4)(a) CPR r. 44.3(1) CPR r. 44.3(1) CPR r. 44.3(2)(a) Macleish v Littlestone, Court of Appeal (2016)

CHAPTER ELEVEN

INTRODUCTION TO DEFENCES

Nota bene – The enclosed defences are not a comprehensive list of possible defences. There are so many permutations that are so case specific that it would be impossible to include every possibility. The important thing to remember is that unless it is a clear-cut case in which you can achieve a dismissal, then if at all possible you should be trying to secure additional time for your client to file a defence. If there looks like there is the possibility of a defence which needs further exploration then this should be enough to secure an adjournment with directions for a Defence to be filed. Do not limit your thinking to the possibilities set out in this guide if there is something that smells fishy but isn't covered.

Nota bene quoque – Whenever you are asking (1) for a dismissal, if the court is not on board with that option (and has discretion to pursue alternative options), then in the alternative ask for (2) directions that a defence may be filed (on the point raised and any others that may become apparent), and if the court is again not on board with this option (and again has discretion to do otherwise), then ask for (3) an adjournment with an order that the claimant correct whatever defect exists by a certain date, with re-filing and re-service by that date, in default of which the claim shall stand struck out without further order. This *nota bene quoque* will most readily apply to some of the technical defences that you might be able to raise.

Nota tum maxime – Wherever a discretion may be used to overcome a defect – such as the discretion contained in CPR r. 3.10 – it should *only* be exercised with a view to furthering the overriding objective. That is, to deal with matters justly and at proportionate cost. Dealing with matters justly includes (among other factors) considering the importance of the case to the parties. The Supreme Court has acknowledged that "the loss of one's home is the most extreme form of interference with the right for respect for the home" (Pinnock v Manchester City Council, Supreme Court (2011)). Possession cases are of the utmost importance to defendants as they face the imminent loss of their home. It may be submitted that – wherever there is an error in the claim – the court's discretion (if it has any) ought not to be used to rectify it because of the overwhelming importance of the case to the Defendant.

CHAPTER TWELVE

GENERAL DEFENCES

STANDING

1. **Does the claimant have standing to bring the claim?**

   (i) Does the named claimant have standing to bring the claim?

   - Only the party entitled to possession in reversion may bring the claim.

     - NOT the landlord's agent on behalf of the landlord (the claimant must have better title to possession than the defendant – there is a "bedrock principle of relativity of title which pervades English land law" (Global 100 Limited v Maria Laleva, Court of Appeal (2021)). A mere agent does not have even the appearance of a right to possession.

   - The landlord as per the tenancy agreement is entitled to bring the claim (regardless of the quality of that party's own title – i.e. this may include the lettings agency if they prepared and signed the tenancy agreement in their own name).

     - The tenant or licensee is estopped from denying the claim of the party which granted them the lease or licence (whether or not that party actually had the right to grant said lease or licence) (Global 100 Limited v Maria Laleva, Court of Appeal (2021)).

- If the landlord as per the tenancy agreement did not have / no longer has the right to possession in reversion, the third party so entitled may also bring the claim for possession.
  - "It almost goes without saying that the fee simple title by estoppel is not binding on anyone who is not estopped. Consequently the true owner would be entitled to show that he had a better title than either of the estopped parties" (Global 100 Limited v Maria Laleva, Court of Appeal (2021)).

(ii) If not, then DEFENCE:

- Only the party entitled to possession in reversion may bring the claim (Global 100 Limited v Maria Laleva, Court of Appeal (2021));
- Claim should be struck out pursuant to CPR r. 55.8(1)(a).

(iii) DISCRETION OF THE COURT:

- None. A claim may not be brought by a party that has no standing.

<u>Global 100 Limited v Maria Laleva, Court of Appeal (2021)</u>

LORD JUSTICE LEWISON: "It almost goes without saying that the fee simple title by estoppel is not binding on anyone who is not estopped. Consequently the true owner would be entitled to show that he had a better title than either of the estopped parties".

"[There is a] bedrock principle of relativity of title which pervades English land law".

"The principle of estoppel as between landlord and tenant has been settled for centuries... If a person with no interest in land purports to grant another a tenancy of it, that person (if let into possession) is estopped from disputing the grantor's title".

"The principle of estoppel as between landlord and tenant applies equally to a licence of land as between licensor and licensee".

2. <u>Is the Claimant named correctly?</u>

(i) Has the claimant been named correctly including with appropriate legal suffixes (e.g. "Limited")

(ii) If not, then DEFENCE:

- The claim must include the claimant's full name including appropriate legal suffix (e.g. "Limited") (PD 16 para. 2.4);
- If there is an error in naming the claimant this requires amendment pursuant to CPR Part 17.

(iii) DISCRETION OF THE COURT:

- If the only problem is that the claimant's name is misspelled or it is a company whose name is not set out correctly (a minor error), the court may give permission to amend it (CPR 17.4(3));
- If, however, the mistake is not minor and there may be doubt as to the identity of the party, permission cannot be given and the issue then becomes an issue of standing (see above).

<u>PD 16 para. 2.4</u>

The claim form must be headed with the title of the proceedings, including the full name of each party, where it is known –

(1) for an individual, the full name and title by which the person is known;

...

(4) for a company or limited liability partnership registered in England and Wales, the full registered name, including suffix (plc, Limited, LLP, etc)...

CPR 17.4(3)

The court may allow an amendment to correct a mistake as to the name of a party, but only where the mistake was genuine and not one which would cause reasonable doubt as to the identity of the party in question.

3. Has the claimant died since bringing the claim?

(i) Have the Personal Representatives successfully applied to be added / be substituted for the claimant in the proceedings?

(ii) If not, then DEFENCE:

- The Personal Representatives cannot simply act as agent for the deceased claimant in the proceedings (agents are unregulated and cannot conduct litigation) and need to be substituted as claimant.

(iii) DISCRETION OF THE COURT:

- On application by the claimant, the court may add or substitute a party (CPR 19.2(4)), but this requires an application under Part 19 and written consent (i.e. it cannot be dealt with on the day);
- If the court chooses not to adjourn to allow such an application, then the issue on the day becomes an issue of who has conduct of the litigation (see below).

CPR 19.2(4)

The court may order a new party to be substituted for an existing one if (a) the existing party's interest or liability has passed to the new party; and (b) it is desirable to substitute the new party so that the court can resolve the matters in dispute in the proceedings.

CPR 19.4(4)

Nobody may be added or substituted as a claimant unless (a) he has given his consent in writing; and (b) that consent has been filed with the court.

CONDUCT OF THE LITIGATION AND RIGHTS OF AUDIENCE

1. **Is the person who is seeking the audience of the court an authorised or exempt person?**

(i) Is the person representing the Claimant at court an authorised or exempt person?

	Definition	Authority
Authorised person	A legal representative regulated by the SRA	s18 Legal Services Act 2007
Exempt person	A litigant in person	s19 and Sch 3 para. 1 (6) Legal Services Act 2007
	A person with the permission of the court	s19 and Sch 3 para. 1 (2) Legal Services Act 2007

(ii) If not, then DEFENCE:

- The exercise of a right of audience is a reserved activity (s12 Legal Services Act 2007);
- Only authorised or exempt persons may carry out a reserved activity (s13 Legal Services Act 2007);
- It is an offence to carry on a reserved activity if not entitled (s14(1) Legal Services Act 2007). Where the activity in question is the exercise of a right of audience, then it may also amount to contempt of court (s14(4) Legal Services Act 2007);
- The claim cannot be heard under such circumstances and should be dismissed.

(iii) DISCRETION OF THE COURT:

- The court may adjourn to give the claimant the chance to attend OR may simply grant the person in attendance a right of audience on the day (Sch 3 para. 1(2)(b) Legal Services Act 2007).

- HOWEVER:

  "Courts should be slow to grant an application from a litigant for a right of audience or a right to conduct litigation to any lay person… This is because a person exercising such rights must ordinarily be properly trained, be under professional discipline (including an obligation to insure against liability for negligence) and be subject to an overriding duty to the court. These requirements are necessary for the protection of all parties to litigation and are essential to the proper administration of justice" (Practice Guidance (McKenzie Friends) (2010), cited by HHJ Worster in Kassam v Gill & Gill, County Court appeal, Birmingham County Court (2018)).

  (This modern guidance is based on caselaw authority (D v S (Rights of Audience), Court of Appeal (1997), confirmed in Paragon Finance plc v Noueiri, Court of Appeal (2001))).

- Following the decision of the Court of Appeal in respect of the conduct of litigation in Ndole Assets Ltd v Designer M&E Services UK Ltd (see section below), I cannot see that a court would be persuaded that it accords with the overriding objective to dismiss the claim for this offence at the first hearing. The best you may be able to achieve is an adjournment. It would seem draconian to dismiss an attended claim for this – but you can try!

- If the court insists on making a possession order then costs should be disallowed (Kassam v Gill & Gill, County Court Appeal, Birmingham County Court (2018)) (see section below).

Sch 3 para. 1 Legal Services Act 2007

(2) The person is exempt if the person—

(a) is not an authorised person in relation to that activity, but

(b) has a right of audience granted by that court in relation to those proceedings.

...

(6) The person is exempt if the person—

(a) is a party to those proceedings, and

(b) would have a right of audience, in the person's capacity as such a party, if this Act had not been passed.

Section 12(1) Legal Services Act 2007

In this Act "reserved legal activity" means—

(a)the exercise of a right of audience;

(b) the conduct of litigation;

...

Section 13(2) Legal Services Act 2007

A person is entitled to carry on an activity ("the relevant activity") which is a reserved legal activity where—

(a) the person is an authorised person in relation to the relevant activity, or

(b) the person is an exempt person in relation to that activity.

Section 14 Legal Services Act 2007

(1) It is an offence for a person to carry on an activity ("the relevant activity") which is a reserved legal activity unless that person is entitled to carry on the relevant activity.

...

(4) A person who is guilty of an offence under subsection (1) by reason of an act done in the purported exercise of a right of audience, or a right to conduct litigation, in relation to any proceedings or contemplated proceedings is also guilty of contempt of the court concerned and may be punished accordingly.

Section 18(1) Legal Services Act 2007

For the purposes of this Act "authorised person", in relation to an activity ("the relevant activity") which is a reserved legal activity, means —

(a) a person who is authorised to carry on the relevant activity by a relevant approved regulator in relation to the relevant activity (other than by virtue of a licence under Part 5), or

(b) a licensable body which, by virtue of such a licence, is authorised to carry on the relevant activity by a licensing authority in relation to the reserved legal activity.

Section 19 Legal Services Act 2007

In this Act, "exempt person", in relation to an activity ("the relevant activity") which is a reserved legal activity, means a person who, for the purposes of carrying on the relevant activity, is an exempt person by virtue of—

(a) Schedule 3 (exempt persons)

...

D v S (Rights of Audience), Court of Appeal (1997)

LORD WOOLF MR: "[The 1990 Act – the predecessor to the Legal Services Act 2007] does give a court a discretion [to give rights of audience in particular proceedings]. In my view it is quite clear from the terms in which the Act as a whole is written that it is giving a discretion which is to be exercised only in exceptional circumstances... [The grant of rights of audience in particular proceedings] is the responsibility of the courts who have been given that responsibility by Parliament. Those who have rights of audience are subject to very stringent requirements".

Paragon Finance plc v Noueiri, Court of Appeal (2001)

LORD JUSTICE BROOKE: "It is clear that we must repeat in this judgment the guidance given by Lord Woolf MR in D v S... [cites and approves as above]".

Gregory & Anor v Turner & Anor, Court of Appeal (2003)

LORD JUSTICE BROOKE: "There is authority that the discretion to allow appearance in particular proceedings (under category (c)) is not intended to override generally the restrictions in the Act [cites and approves Paragon Finance v Noueiri and D v S]".

2. Is the litigation conducted by an authorised or exempt person?

(i) Is the claimant's litigation being conducted by an authorised or exempt person?

	Definition	Authority
Authorised person	A legal representative regulated by the SRA	s18 Legal Services Act 2007
Exempt person	A litigant in person A person with the permission of the court	s19 and Sch 3 para. 2(4) Legal Services Act 2007 s19 and Sch 3 para. 2(2) Legal Services Act 2007

Conduct of litigation includes:

- Sending the claim form by way of service (Ndole Assets Ltd v Designer M&E Services UK Ltd, Court of Appeal (2018));
- Accepting documents by way of service (i.e. the address given for service);
- Verification of the statement of truth on the claim form and the particulars of claim;
- Issuing proceedings;
- Commencement, prosecution and defence of proceedings;
- Ancillary functions in relation to proceedings.

(ii) If not, then DEFENCE:

- Conduct of litigation is a reserved activity (s12 Legal Services Act 2007);

- Only authorised or exempt persons may carry out a reserved activity (s13 Legal Services Act 2007);

- It is an offence to carry on a reserved activity if not entitled (s14(1) Legal Services Act 2007). Where the activity in question is the conduct of litigation, then it is also a contempt of court (s14(4) Legal Services Act 2007).

- For this claim to have been brought in this way may therefore be an abuse of process in which case the claim should be dismissed.

(iii) DISCRETION OF THE COURT:

- If the court is not persuaded to strike out the claim, then it should give directions for a Defence to be filed.

- Although the court may grant permission on an application for permission to conduct litigation (Sch 3 para. 2(2) Legal Services Act 2007), it should be reluctant to do so:

  "Courts should be slow to grant an application from a litigant for a right of audience or a right to conduct litigation to any lay person... This is because a person exercising such rights must ordinarily be properly trained, be under professional discipline (including an obligation to insure against liability for negligence) and be subject to an overriding duty to the court. These requirements are necessary for the protection of all parties to litigation and are essential to the proper administration of justice" (Practice Guidance (McKenzie Friends) (2010), cited by HHJ Worster in Kassam v Gill & Gill, County Court appeal, Birmingham County Court (2018)).

- Following the decision of the Court of Appeal in respect of the conduct of litigation in Ndole Assets Ltd v Designer M&E Services UK Ltd, it may be less likely that a court would be persuaded that it accords with the overriding objective to dismiss the claim for this offence at the first hearing. The best you may be able to achieve is an adjournment. You can certainly try for a dismissal however – especially in cases where the offence committed is more rather than less egregious.

- The fact that various iterations of this question have been taken to the Court of Appeal on more than one occasion should give strong grounding for a submission that directions for a Defence should be given at the very least.

- If the court insists on making a possession order then costs should be disallowed (Kassam v Gill & Gill, County Court Appeal, Birmingham County Court (2018)).

[see other authorities in the section above].

<u>Sch. 3 Para. 2(2) and (4) Legal Services Act 2007</u>

(2) The person is exempt if the person—

(a) is not an authorised person in relation to that activity, but

(b) has a right to conduct litigation granted by a court in relation to those proceedings.

...

(4) The person is exempt if the person—

(a) is a party to those proceedings, and

(b) would have a right to conduct the litigation, in the person's capacity as such a party, if this Act had not been passed.

Ndole Assets Ltd v Designer M&E Services UK Ltd, Court of Appeal (2018)

LORD JUSTICE DAVIS: "The overall conclusion… has to be that formal service of a claim form on a Defendant falls within the "conduct of litigation" for the purposes of the 2007 Act. It is therefore a reserved legal activity which can only be performed by a statutorily authorised person or by an exempt person".

"The consequences of a breach of a statutory provision are, in the ordinary way, to be found in the scheme and terms of the statute itself… In my view, nullity is not to be taken as the statutorily intended consequence [for this breach]… [T]here is no reason why so draconian a consequence should be intended to be visited on the client or principal"… In my judgment, such a conclusion is not acceptable and not compelled by the language of the 2007 Act. Moreover, that does not mean that there is no sanction available. On the contrary there are sanctions available in the form, in an appropriate case, of criminal process and sentence and a contempt application".

"… [it is] an irregularity not a nullity".

Kassam v Gill & Gill, County Court Appeal, Birmingham County Court (2018)

HIS HONOUR JUDGE WORSTER: "It would be neither just nor proportionate to deprive the Claimants of their [claim]. They have committed no wrong. I raised with Mr Walder the question of whether it was appropriate to strike out because that was the only means the court had to prevent this sort of abuse. He submitted that it was a matter for the criminal law, not for this court. Having considered the matter, I agree. The proportionate response would be to disallow costs… There is no discernible effect on the fairness of the trial, and it should not prevent the Claimants proceeding with their claim".

PARTICULARISATION OF THE CLAIM

1. Do the Particulars of Claim set out the grounds for possession?

(i) Do the Particulars of Claim set out the statutory grounds for possession?

(ii) If not, then DEFENCE:

- The Particulars of Claim must state the ground on which possession is claimed (PD 55A para. 2.1(3));
- PoC should be struck out pursuant to CPR 3.4(2)(a);
- Claim should be dismissed pursuant to CPR 55.8(1)(a).

(iii) DISCRETION OF THE COURT:

- On application by the claimant, the court may give permission to amend the Particulars of Claim (CPR 17.1(2)(b))

PD 55A para. 2.1(3)

The Particulars of Claim must state the ground on which possession is claimed.

CPR r. 3.4(2)(a)

The court may strike out a statement of case if it appears to the court… that the statement of case discloses no reasonable grounds for bringing or defending the claim.

CPR r. 17.1(2)(b)

If his statement of case has been served, a party may amend it… with the permission of the court.

2. **Do the Particulars of Claim identify the correct property for which possession is being sought?**

   (i) If not, then DEFENCE as above (requirement: PD 55A para. 2.1(1))

PD 55A para. 2.1(1)

The Particulars of Claim must identify the land to which the claim relates.

3. **Do the Particulars of Claim identify each of the tenants on the tenancy agreement?**

    (i) If not, then DEFENCE as above (requirement: PD 55A para. 2.1(5)).

PD 55A para. 2.1(5)

The Particulars of Claim must give details of every person who, to the best of the claimant's knowledge, is in possession of the property.

COURT FORMS USED

1. **Have the correct (and up-to-date) court forms been used by the claimant?**

   (i) Has Form N5 been used for the Claim Form and Form N119 been used for the PoC, (or N5B for the accelerated procedure) and are these the up-to-date versions?

N5 Claim Form: Versions	Notes
9 February 2021 (current statement of truth)	Labelled on the face as being "10.20" and "Crown Copyright 2020".
6 August 2018	
1 May 2014	

N5B Claim Form: Versions	Notes
11 September 2020 (current statement of truth)	Labelled on the face as being "08.20".
13 August 2018	
10 August 2018	
6 August 2018	
1 August 2017	

N119 PoC: Versions	Notes
9 February 2021 (current statement of truth)	Labelled on the face as being "10.20" and "Crown Copyright 2020".
22 October 2018	
7 August 2018	
1 April 2010	

[Nota Bene – I am unclear as to why the "versions" listed on the Government website are given dates later than those dates stated on the face of them. The current statement of truth was effective from 04.20 so perhaps it makes sense that the forms were actually updated at the earlier dates, but why then list the official version date as a later date?].

(ii) If not, then DEFENCE:

- The forms set out in a practice direction shall be used in the cases to which they apply (CPR r. 4(1));
- The Claimant must use the appropriate claim form and particulars of claim form set out in Table 1 to PD 4 (PD 55A para. 1.5);
- Table 1 identifies N5 and N119 as the required forms;
- This is a breach of the rules of court and sanction should follow. The correct forms are readily available online (after the version date as above) and the claimant should have used them. The court should dismiss the present proceedings;
- Not only is the claimant in breach of the above requirements, but the claim form / PoC is not verified by a valid statement of truth (see section on statements of truth).

(iii) DISCRETION OF THE COURT:

- The court should note that an error of procedure such as a failure to comply with a rule or practice direction does not invalidate any step taken in the proceedings unless the court so orders (CPR r. 3.10(a));
- The court may make an order to remedy the failure to comply with a rule or practice direction (CPR r. 3.10(b)) – this is a broad discretion which should be given wide

effect (Phillips v Symes, House of Lords (2008)), and it "must be exercised in accordance with the overriding objective" (Steele v Mooney & Others, Court of Appeal (2005));

- The key consideration in taking into account the proper administration of justice in respect of using the correct form is whether the Defendant knew what was being claimed and why (Hannigan v Hannigan, Court of Appeal (2000);

- The High Court has applied this reasoning specifically in relation to possession proceedings (Baxendale-Walker v APL Management Ltd, High Court (Chancery Division) (2018));

- The High Court has also found (in an Admiralty context) that using the wrong claim form should not necessarily be fatal to a claim and that dismissal would be disproportionate – but only in a context where the Defendant would thereby receive a "windfall" – e.g. by dismissing the claim any subsequent claim would then be time-barred by limitation (LD Commodoties Rice Merchandising LLC v The Owners and / or Charterers of the Vessel Styliani Z, High Court (Admiralty) (2015));

- The Court of Appeal has held that incurring expense over technicalities out of all proportion to the matters in dispute, and not exercising the discretion in r. 3.10, is the "antithesis of justice" (Hannigan v Hannigan, Court of Appeal (2000)).

- However, a case may be distinguished from the above in light of the overriding objective given the overwhelming importance of a person's home. The High Court decision in Baxendale-Walker v APL Management Ltd is not binding authority and in any event dealt with a mortgaged residential property not one subject to an AST. Further, the Supreme Court in Pinnock v Manchester City Council has confirmed that "the loss of one's home is the most extreme form of interference with the right for respect for the home". And the Admiralty case suggests that dismissing a claim for using the wrong claim form may only be disproportionate if the Defendant would thereby receive some "windfall".

- ALSO: see section on statements of truth.

CPR r. 4(1)

The forms set out in a practice direction shall be used in the cases to which they apply.

PD 55A para. 1.5

The claimant must use the appropriate claim form and particulars of claim form set out in Table 1 to Practice Direction 4.

CPR r. 3.10

Where there has been an error of procedure such as a failure to comply with a rule or practice direction –

(a) the error does not invalidate any step taken in the proceedings unless the court so orders; and

(b) the court may make an order to remedy the error.

LD Commodoties Rice Merchandising LLC v The Owners and / or Charterers of the Vessel Styliani Z, High Court (Admiralty) (2015)

THE HONORABLE MR JUSTICE TEARE: "Where there has been an error of procedure which was culpable and ought never to have happened it can be said, with force, that the court ought not to remedy the error because the court should enforce its rules and thereby encourage careful rather than sloppy practice in the conduct of proceedings. But if by so doing the defendant receives a windfall, namely, the benefit of a time bar defence as a result of inadvertence by the claimant's solicitor, it can be said, with force, that a refusal to remedy the error causes an injustice out of proportion to the fault of the solicitor. In deciding which course best serves the overriding objective of dealing with the case justly these two conflicting arguments have to be weighed in the balance.

<u>**Baxendale-Walker v APL Management Ltd, High Court (Chancery Division) (2018)**</u>

THE HONORABLE MR JUSTICE CARR: "The formalities of CPR 55... should not be ignored. However, it would be wrong to apply a rigid framework which fetters the exercise of the court's discretion".

"Whilst Form N120 must be used according to PD 55A paragraph 1.5, APL has provided all the relevant information required by N120, which it has placed in a different format with some additional material... This defect is therefore clearly not substantive but technical in nature and its rectification would cause no injustice to Mr Baxendale-Walker".

<u>**Phillips v Symes, House of Lords (2008)**</u>

LORD BROWN OF EATON-UNDER-HEYWOOD: [Favourably referenced (in relation to r. 3.10) the majority Court of Appeal decision of LORD JUSTICE McCOWAN and SIR JOHN MEGAW in Golden Ocean Assurance Ltd v Martin, The Goldean Mariner (1990) that the predecessor rule to r. 3.10 (which Lord Brown considered equivalent) to be:] "a most beneficial provision, to be given wide effect".

<u>**Steele v Mooney & Others, Court of Appeal (2005)**</u>

LORD JUSTICE DYSON: "r. 3.10 gives the court a discretion. This must be exercised in accordance with the overriding objective of dealing with cases justly (see r. 1.1(1)). If remedying one party's error will cause injustice to the other party, then the court is unlikely to grant relief under the rule. This gives the court the necessary control to ensure that the apparently wide scope of r. 3.10 does not cause unfairness".

"The general language of r. 3.10 cannot be used to achieve something that is prohibited under another rule. That is the principle established by Vinos's case".

Hannigan v Hannigan, Court of Appeal (2000)

LORD JUSTICE BROOKE: [On DJ Rowley striking out a claim for several purely technical failures including (in particular) the incorrect claim form being used, and HHJ Rubery at the county court appeal declining to exercise discretion under r. 3.9 (relief from sanction) or r. 3.10] "I am in no doubt that the manner in which the judge exercised his discretion was seriously flawed, because he wholly failed to take into account the fact that in these proceedings, sealed by the county court within the relevant limitation period, the defendants were given all the information they required in order to be able to understand what order Mrs Hannigan was seeking from the court and why she was seeking it. He concentrated exclusively on all the technical mistakes Mr Durrell [Mrs Hannigan's solicitor] had made – the lack of a Coat of Arms, the lack of a 3.5cm margin, the absence of the requisite legend in the top right-hand corner of the documents and so on – and in so doing, in my opinion, lost sight of the wood for the trees. The sanction he imposed was also a quite disproportionate response to the procedural irregularities he was considering...

"... In these circumstances it appears to me that this court is not merely entitled, but bound, to exercise its discretion afresh....

"... In my judgment the matter fell technically within CPR r. 3.10 rather than CPR r. 3.9, because the sanction did not flow automatically from any rule, practice direction or court order... [However] I have no doubt that in deciding whether or not to make an order to remedy the relevant errors in circumstances like these the court should take into account each of the factors listed in CPR r. 3.9(1), as far as they are relevant, as well as any other relevant circumstance...

"... One must not lose sight of the fact that the overriding objective of the new procedural code is to enable the court to deal with cases justly, and this means the achievement of justice as between the litigants whose dispute it is the court's duty to resolve. In taking into account the interests of the administration of justice, the factor which appears to me to be of paramount importance in this case is that the defendants and their solicitors knew exactly what was being claimed and why it was being claimed...

"CPR r. 1.3 provides that the parties are required to help the court to further the overriding objective, and the overriding objective is not furthered by and squabbles about technicalities such as have disfigured this litigation and eaten into the quite slender resources available to the parties...

"... Mr Hornby [the claimant's barrister] submitted that... because his clients wished to resist this claim, and there was a potentially valuable limitation point available to them if they succeeded in striking out the proceedings on their chosen ground. I can well understand this attitude, particularly in the early days of the new regime, when it was not widely appreciated that the old turf wars between solicitors over technicalities were being superseded by a new climate in which the emphasis was on the achievement of justice at a cost which was not disproportionate to the matters involved in the dispute. The strategy adopted by the defendants has, however, sadly led to the incurring of expense in ancillary litigation over technicalities which is out of all proportion in relation to what is really in dispute in this case...

"... If we do not make an order directing the correction of these errors... in my judgment the result would be the antithesis of justice... [T]o strike out her claim in these circumstances is a totally disproportionate response to the errors that were made".

VERIFICATION BY STATEMENT OF TRUTH

1. **Have statements of case and statements of fact been verified by the correct statement of truth?**

   (i) Has the claim form, particulars of claim, and any witness statement or certificate of service relied on, been verified by a statement of truth, and is that statement of truth in the up-to-date form?

   (ii) If not, then DEFENCE:

   - A statement of case / witness statement / certificate of service MUST be verified by a statement of truth (CPR r. 22.1(1)(a), (c), (f));

   - The statement of truth should be in the prescribed form (PD 21 paras. 2.1 or 2.2). This new form has been applicable since 6 April 2020 pursuant to the 113th Update to the Civil Procedure Rules.

	Statement of Case (CF / PoC)	**Witness Statement (arguably also certificate of service)**	**Authority**
Wording	"[I believe][the (claimant or as may be) believes] that the facts stated in this [name document being verified] are true. I understand] [The (claimant or as may be) understands that proceedings for contempt of court may be brought against anyone who makes, or causes to be made, a false statement in a document verified by a statement of truth without an honest belief in its truth".	"I believe that the facts stated in this witness statement are true. I understand that proceedings for contempt of court may be brought against anyone who makes, or causes to be made, a false statement in a document verified by a statement of truth without an honest belief in its truth".	PD 21 paras. 2.1 (statements of case) or 2.2 (witness statements)

Consequences of breach	The statement of case may not be relied upon as evidence of any of the matters set out in it (CPR r. 22.2(1)(b)) (though it remains effective unless struck out r. 22.2(1)(a)).	If a witness statement is not validly verified by a statement of truth, the court may direct that it is not admissible as evidence (CPR r. 22.3).	CPR r. 22.2 (statements of case) or r. 22.3 (witness statements)
Submissions to be made	An oral application to strike out the statement of case (CPR r. 22.2(2) and (3)). Also and in any event, the Claimant cannot rely on the contents of a statement of case not verified by a valid statement of truth and so the claim discloses no grounds for possession and should be dismissed.	Invite the court to exercise its discretion to direct that the witness statement is not admissible in evidence. Also make submissions relevant to the claimant being unable (if inadmissible) to rely on the contents of the witness statement (or, perhaps, the certificate of service), and the consequences of this on the overall claim.	(as set out)

[Nota Bene – it is without a doubt that a Certificate of Service has to be verified by a statement of truth. What is not clear is whether that statement of truth has to take one of the prescribed forms. Arguably (to my mind) it should follow the rules of a witness statement, both being statements of fact. However, this is not specified in the Practice Direction. It is worth noting that the template Certificate of Service offered on the Government website (Form N215) contains the wording: "I believe that the facts stated in this certificate are true". There seems to be no concern in Government therefore that certificates of service ought to be caught by the rules relating to prescribed wording (although it did take them 10 months to formalise the updated versions of Forms N5, N5B and N119). On the face of it this position does seem correct, but at the same time it seems to me to be an anomaly that really

does not make any sense. Why would an effort be made to draw the attention of signatories to the dangers of contempt for some documents and not others? Does lying on a certificate of service not amount to contempt? Hardly! Is a certificate of service a less important document? I again hardly think so, given the weight such certificates are given by the courts. To my mind it is arguable that a certificate of service, being a statement of fact in the same way as a witness statement (and indeed being replaceable by a witness statement in every way!), should follow the rules of a witness statement in respect of the statement of truth. That is my penny's worth. I suspect however that when faced with a Government pro forma that has not been updated, such an argument will not get far].

- Since the contents of the statement of case / witness statement / (perhaps) certificate of service cannot be relied on, the claim is [defective in some way] and should be dismissed. In the alternative, the defendant makes an oral application for the claimant to be ordered to verify with a valid statement of truth, and to re-file and re-serve by a certain date, else the claim will stand struck out.

(iii) DISCRETION OF THE COURT:

- The court should note that PD 22 paras. 2.1 and 2.2 state that the statement of truth "should" be as follows – i.e. while the presence of a statement of truth is certainly mandatory, it may be that the precise wording of the statement of truth is not mandatory. I am unaware of any authority on this point. It may be that not using the precise wording set out in the PD does not in fact invalidate a statement of truth;

- The court may order the defaulting party to properly verify with a statement of truth, and any party may apply for such an order (CPR r. 22.4);

- If the court accepts that incorrect wording of the statement of truth invalidates the statement of truth (or indeed if no statement of truth is used at all!) then the court cannot exercise its general broad discretion under CPR 3.10 to overcome this defect because there is a specific sanction written into the rules of court for this breach (and indeed there is a specific mechanism for dealing with this breach i.e. the court ordering proper verification) (both as above), and r.3.10 cannot be used as a "get around" for specific sanctions (Vinos v Marks and Spencer plc, Court of Appeal (2001)) (Baxendale-Walker v APL Management Ltd, High Court (Chancery Division) (2018)).

<u>CPR r. 22.1</u>

(1) The following documents must be verified by a statement of truth –

(a) a statement of case;

…

(c) a witness statement;

…

(f) a certificate of service…

<u>CPR r. 22.2</u>

(1) If a party fails to verify his statement of case by a statement of truth –

(a) the statement of case shall remain effective unless struck out; but

(b) the party may not rely on the statement of case as evidence of any of the matters set out in it.

…

(2) The court may strike out a statement of case which is not verified by a statement of truth.

(3) Any party may apply for an order under paragraph (2).

CPR 22.3

If the maker of a witness statement fails to verify the witness statement by a statement of truth the court may direct that it shall not be admissible as evidence.

CPR 22.4

(1) The court may order a person who has failed to verify a document in accordance with rule 22.1 to verify the document.

(2) Any party may apply for an order under paragraph (1).

PD 22 paras. 2.1 and 2.2

2.1 The form of the statement of truth verifying a statement of case, a response, an application notice, a certificate of reasons or a notice of objections should be as follows:

"[I believe][the (claimant or as may be) believes] that the facts stated in this [name document being verified] are true. I understand] [The (claimant or as may be) understands that proceedings for contempt of court may be brought against anyone who makes, or causes to be made, a false statement in a document verified by a statement of truth without an honest belief in its truth".

2.2 The form of the statement of truth verifying a witness statement should be as follows (and provided in the language of the witness statement):

"I believe that the facts stated in this witness statement are true. I understand that proceedings for contempt of court may be brought against anyone who makes, or causes to be made, a false statement in a document verified by a statement of truth without an honest belief in its truth".

Vinos v Marks and Spencer plc, Court of Appeal (2001)

LORD JUSTICE MAY: "The general words of r. 3.10 cannot extend to enable to court to do what [another rule] specifically forbids... Rule 3.10 concerns correcting errors which the parties have made, but it does not by itself contribute to the interpretation of other explicit rules".

Steele v Mooney & Others, Court of Appeal (2005)

LORD JUSTICE DYSON: "The general language of r. 3.10 cannot be used to achieve something that is prohibited under another rule. That is the principle established by Vinos's case".

2. If signed on behalf of a limited a company or by a legal representative, has the statement of truth been signed in the correct manner?

(i) The correct manner is as follows:

	Who may sign?	**How must they sign?**	**Authority**
Signed on behalf of a limited company	must be signed by a person holding a senior position in the company (PD 22 para. 3.4), namely: A director, the treasurer, secretary, chief executive, manager or other officer of the company or corporation (PD 22 para. 3.5).	Signed in his own name not just the name of the company. Must state the position or office he holds (PD 22 para. 3.4).	PD 22 para. 3.4
Signed by a legal representative	'legal representative' means a – (a) barrister; (b) solicitor; (c) solicitor's employee; (d) manager of a body recognised under section 9 of the Administration of Justice Act 1985; or (e) [an authorised or exempt person] who has been instructed to act for a party in relation to proceedings. CPR r. 2.3(1)	Signed in his own name not just the name of his firm (PD 22 para. 3.10). ... with his own name printed beneath the signature (PD 22 para. 3.9). ... stating his position and the name of his firm (PD 22 para. 3.7).	PD 22 para. 3.7

(i) If not, then DEFENCE:

- The statement of truth verifies the facts set out in the claim and establishes that the claimant – being the person entitled to bring the claim – is in fact desirous of the claim being brought. It is fundamental to the proceedings that the court can be satisfied of these matters. This is why, when the claimant does not sign the statement himself (either because the claimant is not a natural person, or because the claimant has a representative) the rules are strict as to who can verify the matters that require verification;

- In the circumstances, the court cannot be satisfied. The claim must therefore be dismissed;

- In addition, signing the statement of truth amounts to the conduct of litigation which is a reserved activity – a person not entitled to sign is therefore committing an offence (see Conduct of Litigation above);

- [If the correct person has signed, they have just not signed in the correct way:] The form the signature must take is specified in the rules so that the court can be satisfied that an appropriate person – of appropriate position – has verified the statement. In the circumstances, the court cannot be satisfied. The same submissions as above therefore apply].

(ii) DISCRETION OF THE COURT:

- These rules are framed in mandatory wording – "must". The signing is integral to the verification by a statement of truth. For a statement to be verified by a statement of truth therefore it must be signed – and that means it must be properly signed in accordance with the rules – by the right person, in the right way;

- This would suggest that where a statement of truth has not been properly signed – by the right person in the right way – the statement has therefore not been verified by a statement of truth. This reasoning would lead us to the rules surrounding discretion as they apply to cases where there is no statement of truth or it is incorrectly worded (see above), i.e. it would lead us to a place where the discretion of r.3.10 is excluded.

Practice Direction 22, paragraph 3.4

"Where a document is to be verified on behalf of a company or other corporation… the statement of truth must be signed by a person holding a senior position in the company or corporation. That person must state the office or position held".

Practice Direction 22, paragraph 3.5

"Each of the following persons is a person holding a senior position… in respect of a registered company or corporation[:] a director, the treasurer, secretary, chief executive, manager or other officer of the company or corporation".

Practice Direction 22, paragraph 3.7

"Where a party is legally represented, the legal representative may sign the statement of truth on his behalf. The statement signed by the legal representative will refer to the client's belief, not his own. In signing he must state the capacity in which he signs and the name of his firm where appropriate".

Practice Direction 22, paragraph 3.9

"The individual who signs a statement of truth must print his full name clearly beneath his signature".

Practice Direction 22, paragraph 3.10

"A legal representative who signs a statement of truth must sign in his own name and not that of his firm or employer".

COVID NOTICE

1. Has a Covid Notice been filed?

(i) Has a notice been filed with the claim form setting out what knowledge that party has as to the effect of the Coronavirus pandemic on the Defendant and their dependants?

(ii) If not, then DEFENCE:

- It is a requirement to serve such a notice with the claim form (PD 55C para. 6.2);
- Failure to do so is a breach of the rules of court and sanction should follow;
- The claim should be dismissed, or in the alternative should be adjourned and the claimant ordered to file and serve a covid notice failing which the claim stand struck out.

(iii) DISCRETION OF THE COURT:

- The court should note that an error of procedure such as a failure to comply with a rule or practice direction does not invalidate any step taken in the proceedings unless the court so orders (CPR 3.10(a));
- The court may make an order to remedy the failure to comply with a rule or Practice Direction (CPR r. 3.10(b)) – this is a broad discretion which should be given wide effect (Phillips v Symes, Court of Appeal (2008)), and it "must be exercised in accordance with the overriding objective" (Steele v Mooney & Others, Court of Appeal (2005)).

CPR r. 3.10

Where there has been an error of procedure such as a failure to comply with a rule or practice direction –

(a) the error does not invalidate any step taken in the proceedings unless the court so orders; and

(b) the court may make an order to remedy the error.

Practice Direction 55C para. 6.2

In any claim (whether a new claim or a stayed claim) brought on or after 3 August 2020 to which Section II of Part 55 applies the Claimant must file with the claim form for service with it a notice setting out what knowledge that party has as to the effect of the Coronavirus pandemic on the Defendant and their dependants.

Phillips v Symes, House of Lords (2008)

LORD BROWN OF EATON-UNDER-HEYWOOD: [Favourably referenced (in relation to r.3.10) the majority Court of Appeal decision of LORD JUSTICE McCOWAN and SIR JOHN MEGAW in Golden Ocean Assurance Ltd v Martin, The Goldean Mariner (1990) that the predecessor rule to r.3.10 (which Lord Brown considered equivalent) to be:] "a most beneficial provision, to be given wide effect".

Steele v Mooney & Others, Court of Appeal (2005)

LORD JUSTICE DYSON: "r. 3.10 gives the court a discretion. This must be exercised in accordance with the overriding objective of dealing with cases justly (see r. 1.1(1)). If remedying one party's error will cause injustice to the other party, then the court is unlikely to grant relief under the rule. This gives the court the necessary control to ensure that the apparently wide scope of r. 3.10 does not cause unfairness".

SERVICE OF THE NOSP

Don't forget to calculate the date of service, be it actual service (take instruction) or deemed service.

1. **Has the NOSP purportedly been served by a valid method?**

   (i) Was the notice (as pleaded) brought to the attention of the tenant as per the common law OR served by some method specified in the tenancy agreement or imported by statute?

   (ii) If not, then DEFENCE:

   - There is no CPR-based provision for service of NOSPs;
   - Service being a matter of contract therefore, a method of service not agreed between the parties in the contract (and not otherwise allowed for by the common law or otherwise imported by statute) cannot be valid since it falls outside the terms of the contract (this may apply to emailed notices);
   - Service not being valid therefore, the claim must be dismissed.

   (iii) DISCRETION OF THE COURT:

   - Section 8 – Court can dispense with service of a Section 8 notice for most grounds (Section 8(1)(b) Housing Act 1988) but NOT for grounds 7A, 7B, or 8 (Section 8(5) Housing Act 1988).
   - Section 21 – Court has no discretion to dispense with service.

2. **Does the Defendant deny service or put the Claimant to proof of service?**

   (i) Is there a deemed service provision in the tenancy agreement, and is the method of service valid as per that provision? [If a pure deemed service provision is appropriately relied on, the defendant's position is irrelevant. If a partial deemed service provision is appropriately relied on, the defendant will have to prove, beyond a bare denial, that the notice was not in fact received. See relevant earlier chapters, and subsequent defences. If there is no deemed service provision or the one that there is is not appropriately relied on, then continue with this defence].

   (ii) If not, then DEFENCE:

   - If the claimant is unable to rely upon a deemed service provision, then he must fall back on old common law rules about service (Wandsworth v Attwell, Court of Appeal (1995));

   - The claimant must satisfy the court to the civil standard that the notice has been brought to the attention of the defendant;

   - It is not enough for the claimant to prove that he sent the notice by post (which is all a Certificate of Service will speak to), or that he affixed the notice to the door of the property etc., because post can get lost, or anything attached to the door might blow off in the wind (or in the words of my colleague William Flack some well-meaning anarchist down the road might have put it in the bin!). There is no common law rule that just because a notice was posted it was received. See relevant earlier chapters. See in particular the relevant judgment in Heywood v Newcastle-upon-Tyne, Supreme Court (2018).

   - See subsequent defences.

(iii) DISCRETION OF THE COURT:

- Section 8 – Court can dispense with service of a Section 8 notice for most grounds (Section 8(1)(b) Housing Act 1988) but NOT for grounds 7A, 7B, or 8 (Section 8(5) Housing Act 1988).
- Section 21 – Court has no discretion to dispense with service.

3. <u>Where service relies on an express deemed service provision in the tenancy agreement, is this clause appropriately relied on?</u>

(i) Does the express deemed service clause set out the method of service required (for notices sent by the landlord to the tenant), and the time after which service is deemed, and is the method used strictly in line with these rules?

(ii) If not, then DEFENCE:

- The clause does not have the clarity required to amount to a deemed service provision / Any deemed service provision must give a timeframe in which service will be deemed – service cannot be deemed as immediate, nor can it be infinite, as the point of service is communication and immediacy belies communication (other than in cases of direct personal service) and infinity is of no help to the claimant at all!

- OR the method of service used is not in accordance with the express clause and therefore the clause cannot be relied upon.

- Deemed service cannot therefore be relied upon.

4. **<u>Where service relies on Section 196 deemed service, is Section 196 appropriately relied on?</u>**

   (i) Has Section 196 of the Law of Property Act 1925 been expressly incorporated into the tenancy agreement (or is the Claimant otherwise entitled to rely on it – see relevant chapter above), and if so is the method of service used one of the following:

   - Affixing to the house / leaving on the land.
   - Leaving at the last place of abode or address.
   - Sending by registered post, this not being returned as undelivered.

   (ii) If not, then DEFENCE:

   - Without express incorporation, s196 cannot be relied upon / s196 is properly incorporated but the method used is not in accordance with the pure deemed service provisions of s196 / although registered post was used, this was returned as undelivered to the claimant.
   - Deemed service cannot therefore be relied upon.

5. **Where service relies on Section 7 deemed service, is Section 7 appropriately relied on, and does the Defendant deny service?**

(i) Has Section 196 of the Law of Property Act 1925 been expressly incorporated into the tenancy agreement (or is the Claimant otherwise entitled to rely on it – see relevant chapter above), and if so is the method of service used one of the following:

- First class post, properly addressed, pre-paid, and posted.

- [If not appropriately relied on then DEFENCE: without express incorporation of Section 196 Law of Property Act 1925 (or other entitlement to rely on it) the Claimant cannot rely upon Section 7 Interpretation Act 1978 and there is therefore no deemed service provision to rely on. ALSO, if the post is not first class, pre-paid, and posted, then Section 7 may not be relied upon].

(ii) Does the Defendant deny service AND can the Defendant evidence this negative beyond a bare denial (even a bare denial on oath)?

(iii) If so, then DEFENCE:

- Section 7 creates a rebuttable presumption of service – it is not a pure deemed service provision. The Defendant hereby rebuts / wishes to rebut the presumption (must have evidence to rebut);

- Either the claimant must proceed as per the common law rules to demonstrate service, or if he cannot do so, the court should dismiss the claim (if satisfied that service was not effected) or adjourn to allow for a Defence to be filed.

(iv) DISCRETION OF THE COURT:

- Section 8 – Court can dispense with service of a Section 8 notice for most grounds (Section 8(1)(b) Housing Act

1988) but NOT for grounds 7A, 7B, or 8 (Section 8(5) Housing Act 1988).

- Section 21 – Court has no discretion to dispense with service.

6. **Where service relies on common law rules, has service been properly effected in accordance with those rules and is service demonstrated to the civil standard?**

(i) Is there a Witness Statement or Certificate of Service, properly validated with a statement of truth, that speaks to effective personal service, namely that:

- The NOSP was handed to the Defendant;
- The Defendant took control of the notice, however briefly; and
- The nature of the notice was readily apparent.

AND is there evidence of the same?

OR

Is there a Witness Statement or Certificate of Service, properly validated with a statement of truth, that speaks to effective personal service, namely that:

- The Defendant would not accept the NOSP and it was left with or near him; and
- It was explained to him what the NOSP is.

AND is there evidence of the same?

OR

Is there a Witness Statement or Certificate of Service, properly validated with a statement of truth, that speaks to effective common law service (other than personal service), namely that:

- The NOSP was left at the property with the Defendant's agent / servant / spouse / adult child;

- It was explained what the NOSP is; and
- The recipient was instructed to give the NOSP to the Defendant.

AND is there evidence of the same?

(ii) If not, then DEFENCE:

- The Claimant is put to strict proof of service and has not pleaded sufficient evidence to support a finding of service to the civil standard.
- The claim must therefore fail.

(iii) If the method used is the third of the above methods, does the Defendant deny receiving the notice AND can the Defendant evidence this negative beyond a bare denial (even on oath)?

(iv) If so, then DEFENCE:

- The Claimant is put to strict proof of service and has not pleaded sufficient evidence to support a finding of service to the civil standard;
- The claim must therefore fail or be adjourned to allow for a Defence on this point to be filed.

(v) DISCRETION OF THE COURT:

- Section 8 – Court can dispense with service of a Section 8 notice for most grounds (Section 8(1)(b) Housing Act 1988) but NOT for grounds 7A, 7B, or 8 (Section 8(5) Housing Act 1988).
- Section 21 – Court has no discretion to dispense with service.

LIMITATION

1. **Have Section 21 proceedings been issued within the relevant limitation period?**

   (i) Is the issue date on the claim form within the appropriate limitation period from the date of service (deemed or actual) of the Section 21 notice?

Date Section 21 notice served	**Time limit to start court action**	**Authority**
Before 29 August 2020	6 months of service	s.21(4D) Housing Act 1988
Between 29 August 2020 and 31 May 2021	10 months of service	Para 7 Sch 29 Coronavirus Act 2020, as amended by Regulation 3(7)(b) The Coronavirus Act 2020 (Residential Tenancies: Protection from Eviction) (Amendment) (England) Regulations 2020
Between 1 June 2021 and 30 September 2021	8 months of service	Para 7 Sch 29 Coronavirus Act 2020, as amended by Regulation 2(8)(c) The Coronavirus Act 2020 (Residential Tenancies: Protection from Eviction) (Amendment) (England) (No. 2) Regulations 2021
On or after 1 October 2021	6 months of service	s.21(4D) Housing Act 1988

   (ii) If not, then DEFENCE:

   - The proceedings have been begun out of time.
   - Claim should be struck out pursuant to CPR r. 3.4(2)(a).

(iii) DISCRETION OF THE COURT:

- None. Proceedings "may not be begun" after the end of the limitation period (mandatory wording) (Section 21(4D) Housing Act 1988)

Section 21(4D) Housing Act 1988

Subject to subsection (4E), proceedings for an order for possession under this section in relation to a dwelling-house in England may not be begun after the end of the period of six months beginning with the date on which the notice was given under subsection (1) or (4).

Para 7 Sch 29 Coronavirus Act 2020

Section 21 of the Housing Act 1988 (recovery of possession on expiry or termination of assured shorthold tenancy) is to be read, in relation to notices given under subsection (1) or (4) of that section during the relevant period, as if— [AMENDMENTS (a) (b) (c)].

Regulation 3(7)(b) The Coronavirus Act 2020 (Residential Tenancies: Protection from Eviction) (Amendment) (England) Regulations 2020

In paragraph 7 (modification of section 21 of the Housing Act 1988: notice of possession proceedings in relation to assured shorthold tenancies)—

...

(b) after paragraph (b) (and before "and" at the end of the paragraph) insert—

"(ba) in subsection (4D) for "six months" there were substituted "10 months"".

Regulation 2(8)(c) The Coronavirus Act 2020 (Residential Tenancies: Protection from Eviction) (Amendment) (England) (No. 2) Regulations 2021

In paragraph 7 (modification of section 21 of the Housing Act 1988(5): notice of possession proceedings in relation to assured shorthold tenancies)—

...

(c) in paragraph (ba) for "10 months" substitute "8 months".

Nota bene – If the claim form was received by the court at an earlier date, then (contrary to the more familiar rule in PD 7A paragraph 6.1 and Barnes v St Helens Metropolitan Borough Council, Court of Appeal (2006)), in possession proceedings it is not that earlier date that should be considered for limitation purposes. There is a distinction between when proceedings are "brought" and when they are "begun" (Salford City Council v Garner, Court of Appeal (2004)). Proceedings are "brought" for the purposes of the Limitation Act 1980, but for the purposes of limitation in the Housing Act 1988 they are "begun". Justice Morgan states in Ideal Shopping Direct Ltd v Visa Europe Ltd, High Court (Chancery Division) (2020) that: "PD7A paragraph 6.1 repeats that proceedings are started when the court issues a claim form at the request of the claimant. That paragraph goes on to provide that where the claim form as issued was received in the court office on a date earlier than the date it was issued by the court, the claim is "brought" for the purposes of the Limitation Act 1980 and any other relevant statute on that earlier date... Paragraph 6.1 of PD7A shows that the general rule is that the claim is not taken to be issued on the date on which the proposed claim form is received by the court office. The exception provided for by paragraph 6.1 of PD7A applies for the purposes of the Limitation Act 1980 and any other statute which refers to proceedings being "brought" (see Barnes v Helens MBC)... The exception in paragraph 6.1 does not apply where the relevant statute does not refer to the "bringing of proceedings" but refers instead to "the beginning of proceedings" (see Salford City Council v Garner)".

2. **Have Section 8 proceedings been issued within the relevant limitation period?**

   (i) Is the issue date on the claim form within 12 months from the date of service (deemed or actual) of the Section 8 notice?

   (ii) If not, then DEFENCE:

   - The proceedings are begun out of time (s8(3)(c) Housing Act 1988);

   - Claim should be struck out pursuant to CPR 3.4(2)(a).

   (iii) DISCRETION OF THE COURT:

   - None in respect of overlooking the limitation issue. The court "shall not entertain proceedings for possession" outside of the limitation period (mandatory wording) (Section 8(1)(a) Housing Act 1988);

   - If "just and equitable", the court may dispense with service of the Section 8 notice altogether (Section 8(1)(b) Housing Act 1988).

     - BUT NOT in respect of grounds 7A, 7B, or 8 (s8(5) Housing Act 1988).

Section 8(1)(a) Housing Act 1988

The court shall not entertain proceedings for possession of a dwelling-house let on an assured tenancy unless… the proceedings are begun within the time limits stated in the notice in accordance with (3) to (4B) below.

Section 8(1)(b) Housing Act 1988

The court shall not entertain proceedings for possession of a dwelling-house let on an assured tenancy unless… the court considers it just and equitable to dispense with the requirement of such a notice.

Section 8(3)(c) Housing Act 1988

Proceedings will not begin later than twelve months from the date of service of the notice.

Section 8(5) Housing Act 1988

The court may not exercise the power conferred by subsection (1)(b) above if the landlord seeks to recover possession on Ground 7A, 7B or 8 in Schedule 2 to this Act.

SEE ALSO Nota Bene above.

FORM AND SUBSTANCE OF THE NOSP

1. **For Section 21 proceedings, has Form 6A been used, and is it the most up-to-date version of the form (when served), or a form substantially to the same effect?**

   (i) Has the correct form and the up-to-date version been used?

Version dates – FORM 6A	
15 November 2012	
28 October 2015	
1 June 2019	Tenant Fees Act 2019 reflected
8 August 2019	
26 March 2020	
3 April 2020	Revised notes
29 August 2020	Notice periods altered (Covid)
2 September 2020	Outdated information removed
1 June 2021	Notice periods altered (Covid)
1 October 2021	Pre-Covid notice periods restored

What is a Form Substantially to the Same Effect?

It fulfils the statutory purpose of the prescribed form.	Pease v Carter, Court of Appeal (2020)
It is "to the like effect as to its substance", meaning:	Tegerdine v Brooks, Court of Appeal (1977)
a. It includes the same information to understand the nature and consequences of the notice.	Manel v Memon, Court of Appeal (2000)
b. It includes the same information to understand the support available to the tenant.	
c. It includes the same information which is "an important safeguard for the tenant", and which is "intended to operate or have an effect upon" the tenant.	
NOT if it contains an incorrect date	Panayi v Roberts, Court of Appeal (1993)

(ii) If not, then DEFENCE:

- The Secretary of State has prescribed Form 6A as the prescribed form of a Section 21 notice (s21(8) Housing Act 1988) (Reg. 3(fa) The Assured Tenancies and Agricultural Occupancies (Forms) (England) Regulations 2015). This OR a form substantially to the same effect MUST be used.

- Form 6A has not been used / or the form that was used was out-of-date by the time it was used.

- The form that was in fact used is not substantially to the same effect as the prescribed in-date form because it does not fulfil the statutory purpose of the prescribed form (Pease v Carter, Court of Appeal (2020)) (see table above).

- The court is invited to strike out the claim for a failure to serve the proper notice. Alternatively, directions should be made for a defence on the submission that the form used is not substantially to the same effect as the prescribed form.

(iii) DISCRETION OF THE COURT:

- If the court considers that the form served is a form "substantially to the same effect" as the up-to-date Form 6A then the court can determine that s21(8) Housing Act 1988 and Reg. 3(fa) The Assured Tenancies and Agricultural Occupancies (Forms) (England) Regulations 2015 have been complied with.
    - Some problems (such as the wrong date – see table above) do not permit a finding that the form is substantially to the same effect. In such cases, the court may consider whether the problem is an evident error that can be cured under the common law (see section below).
    - The court has no discretion to validate a form in this way just because the defect in the form caused the recipient no detriment in practice – it must actually satisfy itself that the form is substantially to the same effect as the one prescribed (Manel v Memon, Court of Appeal (2000)).
- If the court is not satisfied that the form is substantially to the same effect then it has no power to dispense with service owing to mandatory wording in Section 21(1) and (4) Housing Act 1988 ("shall make an order... if it is satisfied...").

- The rules relating to the type of information that should be included in a notice set out in Manel v Memon (see the table above) are persuasive not binding, as the case may be distinguished as dealing with Section 20 notices in a particular historical context.

<u>Section 21(8) Housing Act 1988</u>

The Secretary of State may by regulations made by statutory instrument prescribe the form of a notice under subsection (1) or (4) given in relation to an assured shorthold tenancy of a dwelling-house in England.

<u>Reg. 3(fa) The Assured Tenancies and Agricultural Occupancies (Forms) (England) Regulations 2015</u>

The forms prescribed... are... for a notice under paragraph (1) or (4) of section 21... Form No. 6A.

<u>Reg. 2 The Assured Tenancies and Agricultural Occupancies (Forms) (England) Regulations 2015</u>

In these Regulations... any reference to a numbered form is a reference to the form bearing that number... or to a form substantially to the same effect.

<u>Tegerdine v Brooks, Court of Appeal (1977)</u>

LORD JUSTICE BRIDGE: "Was the notice served... a notice "substantially to the same effect" as the notice prescribed...? What is the meaning of that phrase? I think its meaning is: "Was the notice to the like effect as to its substance"" [relating to notices under the Landlord and Tenant Act 1954 Act].

<u>Manel v Memon, Court of Appeal (2000)</u>

[On considering the validity of a Section 20 notice, whether it was substantially to the same effect as the prescribed form. A Section 20 notice, in the early days of ASTs, was required to be served before an AST was entered into. If the Section 20 notice was not served – or was not valid – then the

tenancy that was subsequently entered into would be a fully assured tenancy, not an AST].

LORD JUSTICE NOURSE: "What... is the substance of a notice under section 20? ... [I]n 1988, an assured shorthold tenancy was both novel in concept and notably less advantageous to tenants than a tenancy protected by the Rent Acts... In the circumstances, the three bullet points on whose omission Mr Buttimore primarily relies [including] in particular... the exhortation to get prior legal advice and the statement that the giving of the notice by the landlord does not commit the tenant to take the tenancy, can *only* be treated as part of the substance of the notice".

LORD JUSTICE NOURSE: "If a notice is not in a form substantially to the same effect as the prescribed form, it is defective irrespective of whether the defect has caused the tenant prejudice or not".

JUSTICE HOLMAN: "The regulations prescribe the bullet points at the beginning of the notice for a purpose. They include the advice or exhortation [to take advice from a solicitor or a Citizens' Advice Bureau]. They make clear [the nature and consequences of the document]... It seems to me that these bullet points must either be a desirable, but optional, extra or an important safeguard for the proposed tenant... In my view... the regulations clearly include them as an important safeguard for the proposed tenant. They are intended to operate or have an effect upon the proposed tenant. The regulations may tolerate some paraphrasing of the bullet points and may tolerate that they appear in different places on the notice. But, in my judgment, if they, or something like them, are omitted altogether, it becomes impossible to view the notice as being "substantially to the same effect" as the prescribed form.

Pease v Carter, Court of Appeal (2020)

LORD JUSTICE ARNOLD: "... Even if a notice, properly interpreted, does not precisely comply with the statutory requirements, it may be possible to conclude that it is "substantially to the same effect" as a prescribed form if it nevertheless fulfils the statutory purpose. This is so even if [there is] information inserted into or omitted from the form..."

Panayi v Roberts, Court of Appeal (1993)

LORD JUSTICE MANN: "A notice with an incorrect date is not substantially to the same effect as a notice with the correct date..."

2. **<u>For Section 8 proceedings, has Form 3 been used and is it the most up-to-date version of the form (when served), or a form substantially to the same effect?</u>**

   (i) Has the correct form and the up-to-date version been used?

Version dates – FORM 3	
15 November 2012	
28 October 2015	
1 December 2016	
26 March 2020	
29 August 2020	Notice periods altered (Covid)
2 September 2020	Outdated information removed
4 May 2021	"Breathing space" information included
1 June 2021	Notice periods altered (Covid)
3 August 2021	Correction of typographical error
1 October 2021	Pre-Covid notice periods restored

What is a Form Substantially to the Same Effect?

It fulfils the statutory purpose of the prescribed form, meaning:	Pease v Carter, Court of Appeal (2020)
a. It warns the tenant that the landlord is considering seeking an order for possession and to give the tenant time to remedy any default.	Northwood (Solihull) Ltd v Fearne & Ors, Court of Appeal (2022)
b. It is a gateway to proceedings.	
It is "to the like effect as to its substance", meaning:	Tegerdine v Brooks, Court of Appeal (1977)
a. It includes the same information to understand the nature and consequences of the notice.	Manel v Memon, Court of Appeal (2000)
b. It includes the same information to understand the support available to the tenant.	
c. It includes the same information which is "an important safeguard for the tenant", and which is "intended to operate or have an effect upon" the tenant.	
NOT if it contains an incorrect date	Panayi v Roberts, Court of Appeal (1993)

(ii) If not, then DEFENCE:

- Notice served under this section must be in the prescribed form (s8(3) Housing Act 1988);

- Form 3 is the prescribed form of a Section 8 notice (Reg. 3(c) The Assured Tenancies and Agricultural Occupancies (Forms) (England) Regulations 2015). This OR a form substantially to the same effect MUST be used;

- The court is required by the Housing Act 1988 not to entertain possession proceedings under Section 8 unless a notice has been served in the prescribed form (s8(1)(a) Housing Act 1988);

- Form 3 has not been used / or the form that was used was out-of-date by the time it was used;

- The form that was in fact used is not substantially to the same effect as the prescribed in-date form because the notice does not fulfil the statutory purpose of the prescribed form (Pease v Carter, Court of Appeal (2020)) (see table above), being in particular:

    a. To warn the tenant that the landlord is considering seeking an order for possession and to give the tenant time to remedy any default, and

    b. As a gateway to proceedings.

    (Northwood (Solihull) Ltd v Fearne & Ors, Court of Appeal (2022))

- The court is invited to strike out the claim for a failure to serve the proper notice. Alternatively, directions should be made for a defence on the submission that the form used is not substantially to the same effect as the prescribed form.

(iii) DISCRETION OF THE COURT:

- If the court considers that the form served is a form "substantially to the same effect" as the up-to-date Form 3 then the court can determine that s8(3) Housing Act 1988 and Reg. 3(c) The Assured Tenancies and Agricultural Occupancies (Forms) (England) Regulations 2015 have been complied with.

- Using an old version of Form 3 may not be enough to render it invalid especially if the grounds relied on are not affected by the updates to the form – such a form is "substantially to the same effect" (Baz v Steele, Croydon County Court, 23 October 2019 (unreported) (not binding)).

- Some problems (such as the wrong date – see table above) do not permit a finding that the form is substantially to the same effect. In such cases, the court may consider whether the problem is an evident error that can be cured under the common law (see section below).

- The court has no discretion to validate a form in this way just because the defect in the form caused the recipient no detriment in practice – it must actually satisfy itself that the form is substantially to the same effect as the one prescribed (Manel v Memon, Court of Appeal (2000)).

▪ However, if the court is not satisfied of this then it can still dispense with service of a Section 8 notice altogether if it considers it just and equitable to do so (Section 8(1)(b) Housing Act 1988) but NOT for ground 8 (Section 8(5) Housing Act 1988).

▪ The rules relating to the type of information that should be included in a notice set out in Manel v Memon are persuasive not binding, as the case may be distinguished as dealing with Section 20 notices in a particular historical context.

<u>**Section 8(1)(a) Housing Act 1988**</u>

"The court shall not entertain proceedings for possession of a dwelling-house let on an assured tenancy unless… the landlord… has served on the tenant a notice in accordance with this section".

Section 8(3) Housing Act 1988

"A notice under this section is one in the prescribed form".

Reg. 3(c) The Assured Tenancies and Agricultural Occupancies (Forms) (England) Regulations 2015

"The forms prescribed... are... for a notice under section 8... Form No. 3".

Reg. 2 The Assured Tenancies and Agricultural Occupancies (Forms) (England) Regulations 2015

"In these Regulations... any reference to a numbered form is a reference to the form bearing that number... or to a form substantially to the same effect".

Northwood (Solihull) Ltd v Fearne & Ors, Court of Appeal (2022)

LORD JUSTICE LEWISON: "... the purpose of the notice is (a) to warn the tenant that the landlord is considering seeking an order for possession and to give the tenant time to remedy any default and (b) as a gateway to proceedings. Both these purposes were fulfilled by the notice that was in fact given: so the effect of the notice was substantially the same... I would hold therefore that the Section 8 notice was valid".

FURTHER CASE LAW AUTHORITIES: See previous section.

3. **Is there an error in the way Form 3 / Form 6A has been filled out?**

(i) Is there an error in the way the form has been filled out?

(ii) Would this error make the reasonable recipient fail to understand what the notice was meant to convey?

(iii) If yes, then DEFENCE:

- Case law is clear that minor and obvious errors – where the truth of what was supposed to be conveyed would be obvious to the reasonable recipient – do not invalidate a notice. The Court of Appeal gave an example of such an obvious error in Panayi v Roberts, Court of Appeal (1993), such as a "slip of the pen" writing "1793" instead of "1993".

- In assessing whether an error can be "cured" by the court, the court should apply a two-part test (York v Casey, Court of Appeal (1998)):

    a. Is the error obvious or evident?

    b. Notwithstanding the error, is the notice read in its context sufficiently clear to leave a reasonable recipient in no reasonable doubt as to the terms of the notice?

- Once the court has determined how a reasonable recipient would interpret the notice, the court is bound by case law authority to adopt that interpretation (Pease v Carter, Court of Appeal (2020)).

- The error in this case is not obvious, OR while the fact that there has been an error may be obvious the real intended meaning of the notice has been sufficiently obscured such that the reasonable recipient would fail to understand what exactly the notice was meant to convey.

- It is therefore submitted that the notice served is invalid and cannot be relied upon.

- The court is invited to strike out the claim for a failure to serve notice. Alternatively, directions should be made for a defence on the submission that the notice is invalid.

(iv) DISCRETION OF THE COURT:

- It is a finding of fact for the court to determine whether or not the error is obvious or would obscure the information that the notice is trying to convey to the reasonable person. The court may consider the contents of any covering letter when determining whether or not the error was obvious and whether or not it was obfuscatory in context (York v Casey, Court of Appeal (1998)).

- If the error is obvious and does not obscure the meaning of the notice then this will not affect the validity of the notice (Northwood (Solihull) Ltd v Fearne & Ors, Court of Appeal (2022)).

- Even if the error cannot be cured in this way per the common law, nonetheless the court may proceed to find that the effect of the notice is substantially the same and therefore satisfies the legislative requirements in any event (see above) (Northwood (Solihull) Ltd v Fearne & Ors, Court of Appeal (2022)) (Pease v Carter, Court of Appeal (2020)).

Pease v Carter, Court of Appeal (2020)

LORD JUSTICE ARNOLD: "The conclusions which I draw... are as follows:

(i) A statutory notice is to be interpreted in accordance with Mannai v Eagle, that is to say, as it would be understood by a reasonable recipient reading it in context.

(ii) If a reasonable recipient would appreciate that the notice contained an error, for example as to date, and would appreciate what meaning the notice was intended to convey, then that is how the notice is to be interpreted.

(iii) It remains necessary to consider whether, so interpreted, the notice complies with the relevant statutory requirements. This involves considering the purpose of those requirements.

(iv) Even if a notice, properly interpreted, does not precisely comply with the statutory requirements, it may be possible to conclude that it is "substantially to the same effect" as a prescribed form if it nevertheless fulfils the statutory purpose".

Northwood (Solihull) Ltd v Fearne & Ors, Court of Appeal (2022)

LORD JUSTICE LEWISON: "In the present case the notice under Section 8 was signed by an authorised agent of the landlord. That complies both with the primary legislation and the prescribed form. The only conceivable error is that Ms Miles crossed out the wrong part of the rubric under her signature [she selected "landlord"]... [however, as the landlord was a company] by definition she personally cannot be the landlord. If it is suggested that the notice purports to describe her personally as the landlord... that is... the sort of obvious error that does not affect the validity of the notice. But even if the error cannot be cured in that way [such as, if the landlord were a natural person], the effect of the notice is substantially the same".

York v Casey, Court of Appeal (1998)

LORD JUSTICE GIBSON: "... the test... accords with the test found to be appropriate in the Panayi case. Accordingly, what the court must do is to see whether the error in the notice was obvious or evident and, second, whether notwithstanding that error the notice read in its context is sufficiently clear to leave a reasonable recipient in no reasonable doubt as to the terms of the notice... I do not accept for one moment that any reasonable recipient of the letter and notice would [not be clear as to the terms of the notice]... To my mind the letter makes clear beyond doubt... what was contemplated".

<u>**Panayi v Roberts, Court of Appeal (1993)**</u>

LORD JUSTICE MANN: "By "evident error" I mean an error which would have been evident to a person with the ordinary qualities of the addressee. I would exclude a quality of obtuseness as being extraordinary. The writing of "1793" for "1993" would be an evident error".

4. **For Form 3, have the grounds for possession been set out?**

   (i) Have the grounds for possession been set out in the notice as they appear in statute (or to the same effect) AND have they been particularised?

   (ii) If not, then DEFENCE:

   - The notice must set out the grounds relied upon and the particulars of each ground – if a ground is not set out then it cannot be relied upon (s8(2) Housing Act 1988). It must be set out with the statutory wording OR with wording substantially to the same effect ((1) Mountain v Hastings, Court of Appeal (1993), Masih v Yousaf, Court of Appeal (2014)).

   - If the ground is listed but the particulars of the ground have not been set out as per the statute (or to the same effect), then the notice itself is invalid (i.e. the notice is not "saved" for the purposes of the grounds that have been properly particularised ((2) Mountain v Hastings, Court of Appeal (1993), Kassam v Gill & Gill, County Court Appeal, Birmingham County Court (2018)).

   - The notice must further particularise how those grounds apply in the circumstances (Torridge v Jones, Court of Appeal (1985)).

Defect	Consequence	Authority
The ground relied upon has not been listed in the Section 8 notice	The ground cannot be relied upon	s8(2) Housing Act 1988
Any ground listed in the Section 8 notice has not been set out with the exact statutory wording or wording to the same effect	The Section 8 notice itself is invalid	Mountain v Hastings, Court of Appeal (1993) Kassam v Gill & Gill, County Court Appeal, Birmingham County Court (2018)
The notice does not explain (particularise) how the ground applies	The Section 8 notice itself is invalid	Torridge v Jones, Court of Appeal (1985)

- The ground has not been listed / has not been particularised, and therefore cannot be relied upon OR the notice is invalid. The claim should be dismissed for failure to serve valid notice. [If the ground has been particularised but not fully particularised, then it should be argued that it has not been sufficiently particularised, meaning that the notice is invalid].

(iii) DISCRETION OF THE COURT:

- If the grounds have been particularised but not fully particularised (both in terms of explaining the grounds, and explaining how they apply in the circumstances), it is a question for the courts as to whether the particularisation is sufficient to consider the notice valid. The court may consider this question in terms of (i) has an error been made, or (ii) is the notice substantially to the same effect as a fully completed notice as prescribed? (for both methods, see sections above).

- If the court is satisfied that the grounds have been sufficiently particularised for the notice to be considered valid, then the court may proceed to give permission (if requested) for the grounds in the notice to be altered or added to (s8(2)HA 1988).
    - This includes giving permission to add to the particularisation of the ground (such as to include a rent statement) (Marath and Anor v Macgillivray, Court of Appeal (1996)).
    - Remember, however, that if the notice is not valid in the first place then the court cannot exercise its discretion under section 8(2) to "cure" it by allowing the claimant to add to it or amend it ((2) Mountain v Hastings, Court of Appeal (1993)).
- The court can still dispense with service of a Section 8 notice altogether if it considers it just and equitable to do so (Section 8(1)(b) Housing Act 1988) but NOT for ground 8 (Section 8(5) Housing Act 1988).

<u>**Section 8 Housing Act 1988**</u>

...

(2) The court shall not make an order for possession on any of the grounds in Schedule 2 to this Act unless that ground and particulars of it are specified in the notice under this section; but the grounds specified in such a notice may be altered or added to with the leave of the court.

...

<u>**Mountain v Hastings, Court of Appeal (1993)**</u>

(1) LORD JUSTICE GIBSON: "As to the submission that the notice was defective because ground 8 was not specified by the full text of that ground as set out in Schedule 2, I do not decide this issue upon that basis. I prefer the view that the ground in Schedule 2 may be validly "specified

in the notice" as required by Parliament, in words different from which the ground is set out in the schedule, provided that the words used set out fully the substance of the ground so that the notice is adequate to achieve the legislative purpose of the provision. That purpose, in my judgment, is to give to the tenant the information which the provision requires to be given in the notice to enable the tenant to consider what she should do and, with or without advice, to do that which is in her power and which will best protect her against the loss of her home".

(2) LORD JUSTICE GIBSON: "Subsection (2) does not, in my judgment, enable the court to [validate] a notice by altering grounds specified. The language of this subsection is directed to a different matter. It assumes that there is a "notice under this section", i.e. a notice which satisfies the requirements of the section… Mr Nance [for the claimant] was driven to concede that, if his client's notice had contained reference only to ground 8 in the form in which it appeared in the notice, and if that form is defective, the court could not dispense with the requirement and the court could not therefore reach subsection (2) in order to "alter" the form in which the ground was specified [to add additional grounds]. But he argued that, since the notice contained other grounds validly specified, the court has jurisdiction to make the "alteration" [to correct the particularisation of ground 8]. That submission seemed to me to be impossible of acceptance for the following reasons. If a landlord serves a notice of intention to begin proceedings for possession of the dwelling-house on more than one ground… then each ground must be specified in the notice. If one ground is not [properly] specified, the notice is not a "notice under this section". There would then be no jurisdiction to entertain the proceedings because no "notice in accordance with this section" has been served unless the court is persuaded to dispense with the requirement of such a notice under subsection (1).

Kassam v Gill & Gill, County Court Appeal, Birmingham County Court (2018)

[The Section 8 notice cited Ground 8, but the citation of this ground omitted the words "and for the purpose of this ground "rent" means rent lawfully due from the tenant"].

HIS HONOUR JUDGE WORSTER: "This notice does not contain the assertion that the amount was lawfully due or owed at the date of the hearing. I conclude that this notice is invalid and the claim under Ground 8 cannot succeed".

Marath and Anor v Macgillivray, Court of Appeal (1996)

SIR IAIN GLIDWELL: "I do not accept the argument… that the court may not allow particulars (in this case the schedule of rent) to be added under s8(2) as a matter of discretion if they have not been given earlier. The section specifically allows added grounds to be given, or alterations to be made and, in my view, giving particulars comes within the subsection".

Torridge District Council v Jones, Court of Appeal (1985)

[This case may be distinguished as it related to a notice to determine a secure tenancy. However, it may be helpful in resisting applications to amend the particulars for Ground 8 claims].

LORD JUSTICE OLIVER: "… for my part I find myself wholly unpersuaded that the mere recitation, almost in the same words, of a part of the ground of which particulars are required to be given can amount to the particulars within the section. I cannot think the legislature can have intended that. It seems to me that it is plain that this subsection does require a specification sufficient to tell the tenant what it is he has to do to put matters right before proceedings are commenced… In my judgment, therefore, the notice which was served… was not a proper notice".

Masih v Yousaf, Court of Appeal (2014)

"It is settled law that the notice does not have to recite verbatim the statutory words of the ground, see Mountain v Hastings (1993)".

5. <u>Who has signed the NOSP?</u>

There is not much to be dealt with in this section other than to state that the position as to some ongoing questions has been clarified recently in Northwood (Solihull) Ltd v Fearne & Ors, Court of Appeal (2022).

The landlord may sign (of course). If joint landlords, only one need sign (with the agreement of the others) (s21(1)(b) Housing Act 1988 / s8(1)(a) Housing Act 1988).

The landlord's agent may sign, in his own name and with his own contact details. The landlord's name and address do not need to be on the form at all (Prempeh v Lakhany, Court of Appeal (2020)).

The agent signing can most likely even put the landlord's name instead of his own (Northwood (Solihull) Ltd v Fearne & Ors, Court of Appeal (2022)).

If the landlord is a company, the notice does not need to be signed in accordance with Section 44 Companies Act 2006. It also does not need to be signed by a director – an authorised employee is sufficient (Northwood (Solihull) Ltd v Fearne & Ors, Court of Appeal (2022)).

If there are any errors in respect of who has signed the NOSP, it is almost inconceivable that Court of Appeal authority would not lead to the conclusion that either the error can be cured via common law rules (see the section on errors, above), or if it cannot be cured in such a way then the form should be considered nonetheless a form "substantially to the same effect" as the prescribed form (again, see the relevant sections above). HOWEVER, as always, if there is a potential defence that does not have a completely clear answer, then ask for directions for a defence.

<u>Northwood (Solihull) Ltd v Fearne & Ors, Court of Appeal (2022)</u>

LORD JUSTICE LEWISON: "The primary legislation governing notice given under section 8 of the Housing Act 1988 does not require signature of anything. It merely requires "service" by the landlord of a notice in a particular form… It follows, in my judgment, that on the face of it a landlord complies with section 8 if an agent serves notice on his behalf, even if the agent signs the notice in the landlord's name. In addition, the form prescribed by the relevant regulations explicitly allows notice to be given by and signed by an agent for the landlord".

Prempeh v Lakhany, Court of Appeal (2020)

LORD JUSTICE NUGEE: "Form 3 [N.B. Form 6A is drafted in the same way] does not require the landlord's own name and address to be provided. It is sufficient that the name and address of the person signing be provided, which may be, as in this case, the agent of the landlord" [This conclusion is based primarily on a plain reading of how the prescribed form is drafted].

NOTICE PERIOD

1. **Did the Section 21 notice give the required notice period?**

(i) At the date of service (actual or deemed) of the Section 21 notice, was the required notice period given by the notice (as per the table below)?

Date Section 21 notice served	**Notice Period**	**Authority**
Before 26 March 2020	2 months of service	s.21(1) Housing Act 1988
Between 26 March 2020 and 28 August 2020 inclusive	3 months of service	Para 7 Sch 29 Coronavirus Act 2020
Between 29 August 2020 and 31 May 2021 inclusive	6 months of service	Para 7 Sch 29 Coronavirus Act 2020, as amended by Regulation 3(7)(a) The Coronavirus Act 2020 (Residential Tenancies: Protection from Eviction) (Amendment) (England) Regulations 2020
Between 1 June 2021 and 30 September 2021 inclusive	4 months of service	Para 7 Sch 29 Coronavirus Act 2020, as amended by Regulation 2(8)(a) The Coronavirus Act 2020 (Residential Tenancies: Protection from Eviction) (Amendment) (England) (No. 2) Regulations 2021
On or after 1 October 2021	2 months of service	s.21(1) Housing Act 1988

(iii) If not, then DEFENCE:

- It is a mandatory requirement that the Section 21 notice give the requisite period of notice (s21(1) Housing Act 1988).

- The Section 21 notice is therefore invalid and the claim must be dismissed.

(iv) DISCRETION OF THE COURT:

- None. Mandatory wording – “not less than”, and “shall” (s21(1) Housing Act 1988).

- No discretion to dispense with service of a Section 21 notice.

- The court does not have a discretion to “cure” a short notice period by noting that proceedings were only commenced after a delay such that the correct amount of time was in fact given. The notice period is what is written in the notice (Pease v Carter, Court of Appeal (2020), obiter).

Section 21(1) Housing Act 1988

… a court shall make an order for possession of the dwelling-house if it is satisfied—

…

(b) the landlord… has given to the tenant not less than two months’ notice…

Para 7 Sch 29 Coronavirus Act 2020

Section 21 of the Housing Act 1988… is to be read… as if—

(a) in subsection (1)(b) for “two months’” there were substituted “three months’”.

…

The Coronavirus Act 2020 (Residential Tenancies: Protection from Eviction) (Amendment) (England) Regulations 2020

Reg. 3(7) In paragraph 7…

(a) in paragraph… (a)… for ""three months"" substitute ""six months"".

…

The Coronavirus Act 2020 (Residential Tenancies: Protection from Eviction) (Amendment) (England) (No. 2) Regulations

Reg. 2(8) In paragraph 7…

(a) in paragraph (a) for "six months'" in the first place it occurs substitute "four months'".

…

Pease v Carter, Court of Appeal (2020)

LORD JUSTICE ARNOLD: [obiter] "In the event, proceedings were not commenced until a further month had elapsed, but in my view that is an irrelevant consideration, because the landlord might have commenced proceedings on 27 November 2018 [the day after the expiry of the notice]".

2. **Did the Section 8 notice give the required notice period?**

   (i) At the date of service (actual or deemed) of the Section 8 notice, was the required notice period given by the notice (as per the table below)?

Date Section 8 notice served	Notice Period	Authority
Before 26 March 2020	**Grounds 8, 10 or 11** – 2 weeks of service	S8(4B) Housing Act 1988
Between 26 March 2020 and 28 August 2020 inclusive	**Grounds 8, 10 or 11** – 3 months of service	Para. 6(d) Sch. 29 Coronavirus Act 2020
Between 29 August 2020 and 31 May 2021 inclusive	**Grounds 8, 10 or 11** – (a) 4 weeks where arrears are at least 6 months	S8(4BA)(c) Housing Act 1988, and Para. 6(d) and (e) Sch. 29 Coronavirus Act 2020, both as inserted by Reg. 3(6)(c) and (d) The Coronavirus Act 2020 (Residential Tenancies: Protection from Eviction) (Amendment) (England) Regulations 2020
	(b) 6 months where arrears are less than 6 months at the date of service of the notice	S8(4BA)(a)(ii) Housing Act 1988, and Para. 6(d) and (e) Sch. 29 Coronavirus Act 2020, both as inserted by Reg. 3(6)(c) and (d) The Coronavirus Act 2020 (Residential Tenancies: Protection from Eviction) (Amendment) (England) Regulations 2020
Between 1 June 2021 and 31 July 2021 inclusive	**Grounds 8, 10 or 11** –	Reg. 2(7)(a) The Coronavirus Act 2020 (Residential Tenancies: Protection from Eviction) (Amendment) (England) (No. 2) Regulations 2021

	a) 4 weeks where arrears are at least 4 months	
	b) 4 months where arrears are less than 4 months	Reg. 2(7)(a) and (b) The Coronavirus Act 2020 (Residential Tenancies: Protection from Eviction) (Amendment) (England) (No. 2) Regulations 2021
Between 1 August 2021 and 30 September 2021 inclusive	<u>**Grounds 8, 10 or 11**</u> – a) 4 weeks where arrears are at least 4 months	Reg. 2(7)(a) The Coronavirus Act 2020 (Residential Tenancies: Protection from Eviction) (Amendment) (England) (No. 2) Regulations 2021
	b) 2 months where arrears are less than 4 months	Reg. 2(7)(a) and (b) The Coronavirus Act 2020 (Residential Tenancies: Protection from Eviction) (Amendment) (England) (No. 2) Regulations 2021
On or after 1 October 2021	<u>**Grounds 8, 10 or 11**</u> – 2 weeks of service	S8(4B) Housing Act 1988

(ii) If not, then DEFENCE:

- The appropriate notice period is a mandatory requirement and the claim should be dismissed.

(iii) DISCRETION OF THE COURT:

- None in respect of overlooking the notice period. The court "shall not entertain proceedings for possession" unless notice served in accordance with Section 8 (mandatory wording) (Section 8(1)(a) Housing Act 1988).

- However, if "just and equitable", the court may dispense with service of the Section 8 notice altogether (Section 8(1)(b) Housing Act 1988).
    - BUT NOT in respect of grounds 7A, 7B, or 8 (s8(5) Housing Act 1988).
- The court does not have a discretion to "cure" a short notice period by noting that proceedings were only commenced after a delay such that the correct amount of time was in fact given. The notice period is what is written in the notice (Pease v Carter, Court of Appeal (2020), obiter).

<u>**Section 8(4B) Housing Act 1988**</u>

... the date specified in the notice... shall not be earlier than the expiry of the period of two weeks from the date of the service of the notice

<u>**Para. 6 Sch. 29 Coronavirus Act 2020**</u>

Section 8 of the Housing Act 1988... is to be read... as if—

...

(d) in subsection (4B) for "two weeks" there were substituted "three months".

<u>**Reg. 3(6)(c) The Coronavirus Act 2020 (Residential Tenancies: Protection from Eviction) (Amendment) (England) Regulations 2020**</u>

...

(c) in paragraph [6(d) Sch. 29 Coronavirus Act 2020] for ""three months"" substitute ""the relevant notice period"

(d) after paragraph (d) insert—

"(e) after subsection (4B) there were inserted in relation to a dwelling-house in England—

[s8(4BA) Housing Act 1988]".

S8(4BA) Housing Act 1988, as inserted by Reg. 3(6)(d) The Coronavirus Act 2020 (Residential Tenancies: Protection from Eviction) (Amendment) (England) Regulations 2020

In subsection… (4B) [to s8 Housing Act 1988], "relevant notice period" means—

(a) where –

…

(ii) any of Grounds 8, 10 or 11 in Schedule 2 to this Act is specified in the notice and at the time the notice is served less than six months' rent is unpaid,

Six months.

…

(c) where paragraph (a)… [does] not apply and any of Grounds 8, 10 or 11 in Schedule 2 to this Act are specified in the notice, four weeks.

…

Reg. 2(7) The Coronavirus Act 2020 (Residential Tenancies: Protection from Eviction) (Amendment) (England) (No. 2) Regulations 2021

(a) in paragraph (a)(ii) [of s8(4BA Housing Act 1988) for "six months' rent" substitute "four months' rent"

(b) in the full out words in paragraph (a) for "six months" substitute — "two months (in the case of a notice served on or after 1 August 2021 in which any of Grounds 8, 10 or 11 is specified and no other ground) or four months (in any other case).

Pease v Carter, Court of Appeal (2020)

LORD JUSTICE ARNOLD: [obiter] "In the event, proceedings were not commenced until a further month had elapsed, but in my view that is an irrelevant consideration, because the landlord might have commenced proceedings on 27 November 2018 [the day after the expiry of the notice]".

LACK OF CAPACITY

1. **Is there doubt as to the Defendant's capacity to litigate?**

   (i) Do you have reasonable doubts as to the Defendant's capacity to understand, retain, use or weigh, and communicate information relevant to the proceedings, and might this be as a result of an impairment of or disturbance in the brain?

   (ii) If so, then DEFENCE:

   - It appears that the Defendant may be a protected party pursuant to CPR r. 21.1(2) in that he may lack capacity to conduct the proceedings (CPR r. 21.1(2)(d).

   - The test for CPR Part 21 is that contained in Section 2(1) of the Mental Capacity Act 2005.

   - I have reasonable doubts as to the ability of the Defendant make a decision for himself pursuant to s3(1) Mental Capacity Act 2005, and that this may be as a result of an impairment of or a disturbance in the brain.

   - It is necessary, where reasonable doubt has been raised, for the court to establish whether the Defendant does lack capacity or suffers from reduced capacity, before proceeding under a presumption of capacity (Mr & Mrs Z v Kent County Council, Family Court at Bromley (2018)).

   - The case should be adjourned so that an expert assessment may be carried out to establish the Defendant's capacity to litigate (or otherwise) and if it is found that he lacks capacity then it will be necessary for a litigation friend to be appointed in line with CPR Part 21.

   - [As an officer of the court it is your duty to bring doubts as to capacity to the attention of the court as soon as possible (RP v Nottingham City Council, Court of Appeal (2007))].

(iii) DISCRETION OF THE COURT:

- None. Capacity to litigate is a fundamental requirement and is a question of fact for the court to determine to the civil standard on evidence (Carmarthenshire County Council v Peter Lewis, Court of Appeal (2010)).

<u>CPR r. 21.1(2)(d)</u>

'protected party' means a party, or an intended party, who lacks capacity to conduct the proceedings.

<u>Section 2(1) Mental Capacity Act 2005</u>

... a person lacks capacity in relation to a matter if at the material time he is unable to make a decision for himself in relation to the matter because of an impairment of, or a disturbance in the functioning of, the mind or brain.

<u>Section 3(1) Mental Capacity Act 2005</u>

For the purposes of section 2, a person is unable to make a decision for himself if he is unable—

(a) to understand the information relevant to the decision,

(b) to retain that information,

(c) to use or weigh that information as part of the process of making the decision, or

(d) to communicate his decision (whether by talking, using sign language or any other means).

Mr & Mrs Z v Kent County Council, Family Court at Bromley (2018)

HER HONOUR JUDGE LAZARUS: "One significant intention [of the presumption of capacity] is to prevent inaccurately assuming lack of capacity in apparently vulnerable individuals without being properly established on evidence. It is emphatically not there to obviate an examination of such an issue. Nor can it have been Parliament's intention to place a vulnerable person in danger of their lack of capacity being overlooked at the expense of their rights by a slack reliance on this presumption".

RP v Nottingham City Council, Court of Appeal (2007)

LORD JUSTICE WALL: "Both the relevant rules of court and the leading case of Masterman-Lister make it clear that once either counsel or [the solicitor] had formed the view that RP might not be able to give them proper instructions, and might be a person under a disability, it was their professional duty to have the question resolved as quickly as possible".

Carmarthenshire County Council v Peter Lewis, Court of Appeal (2010)

LORD JUSTICE RIMER: "In my view the problem raised by this case is as to how, once the court is possessed of information raising a question as to the capacity of the litigant to conduct the litigation, it should satisfy itself as to whether the litigant does in fact have sufficient capacity. I cannot think that the court can ordinarily, by its own impression of the litigant, safely form its own view on that".

EQUALITY ACT DEFENCES

1. Is the tenant being evicted as a result of the landlord's discrimination against a protected characteristic?

(i) Does the Defendant possess a protected characteristic and have the proceedings been commenced as a result of discrimination against this protected characteristic?

The protected characteristics (as they apply to property management decisions):

- disability;
- gender reassignment;
- pregnancy and maternity;
- race;
- religion or belief;
- sex;
- sexual orientation.

(ii) If so, then DEFENCE:

- It is unlawful for a landlord to discriminate against his tenant by seeking eviction on account of one of the relevant protected characteristics (set out above) (s35(1)(b) Equality Act 2010)).
- If the protected characteristic is disability, then it is unlawful for a landlord to seek eviction because of something arising in consequence of the tenant's disability (such as, perhaps, rent arrears or anti-social behaviour) unless the landlord can show that eviction is a proportionate means of achieving a legitimate aim

(reducing rent arrears or ending anti-social behaviour is a legitimate aim, but is eviction proportionate? Is there an alternative available?) (s15 Equality Act 2010).

- If the protected characteristic is pregnancy or maternity, it is unlawful for a landlord to seek eviction because the tenant is pregnant, or because the tenant has given birth within the previous 26 weeks (s17(2) and (3) Equality Act 2010).

- The case should be adjourned and directions given for a Defence.

(iii) DISCRETION OF THE COURT:

- If the claim is disputed on grounds which appear to be substantial, then the court has no discretion but to adjourn and give directions for a Defence.

Section 15 Equality Act 2010

(1) A person (A) discriminates against a disabled person (B) if—

(a) A treats B unfavourably because of something arising in consequence of B's disability, and

(b) A cannot show that the treatment is a proportionate means of achieving a legitimate aim.

(2) Subsection (1) does not apply if A shows that A did not know, and could not reasonably have been expected to know, that B had the disability.

Section 17(2) and (3) Equality Act 2010

(2) A person (A) discriminates against a woman if A treats her unfavourably because of a pregnancy of hers.

(3) A person (A) discriminates against a woman if, in the period of 26 weeks beginning with the day on which she gives birth, A treats her unfavourably because she has given birth.

Section 35(1) Equality Act 2010

A person (A) who manages premises must not discriminate against a person (B) who occupies the premises—

(a) in the way in which A allows B, or by not allowing B, to make use of a benefit or facility;

(b) by evicting B (or taking steps for the purpose of securing B's eviction);

(c) by subjecting B to any other detriment.

CHAPTER THIRTEEN

SECTION 21 SPECIFIC DEFENCES

SERVICE OF THE NOTICE IN THE FIRST 4 MONTHS OF THE TENANCY AGREEMENT

1. **Was the Section 21 Notice served within the first 4 months of the ORIGINAL tenancy agreement?**

(i) Regardless of any purported break clause, and regardless of the length of the initial tenancy, was the Section 21 Notice SERVED within the first four months of the commencement of the ORIGINAL (not replacement) tenancy?

(ii) If yes, then DEFENCE:

- A Section 21 Notice "may not be given" within the first 4 months of the start of the initial tenancy (mandatory wording) (s21(4B) Housing Act 1988).

(iii) DISCRETION OF THE COURT:

- None. Mandatory wording in statute, and service of the notice cannot be dispensed with.

Section 21(4B) Housing Act 1988

A notice under subsection (1) or (4) may not be given in relation to an assured shorthold tenancy of a dwelling-house in England—

(a) in the case of a tenancy which is not a replacement tenancy, within the period of four months beginning with the day on which the tenancy began, and

(b) in the case of a replacement tenancy, within the period of four months beginning with the day on which the original tenancy began.

EXPIRY OF THE NOTICE AND/OR ISSUE OF PROCEEDINGS WITHIN THE CONTRACTUAL PERIOD (INCLUDING BREAK CLAUSES)

1. **Did the Section 21 notice expire, and / or were proceedings issued, within the contractual period without the benefit of a break clause?**

   (i) Does the Notice require possession after a date that is still within the contractual fixed term, such date being without the benefit of a break clause in that contract, and / or were proceedings issued within the contractual period?

   (ii) If yes, then DEFENCE:

   - The landlord is contractually bound to the terms of the agreement and is therefore in breach of contract by serving notice requiring possession within the contractual term without the benefit of a break clause.

   - It is an abuse of process for the claimant to rely on such a notice in breach of contract and the courts cannot be expected to give legal effect to a breach of contract.

     And / Or

   - It is an abuse of process for the claim to have been issued by the Claimant at a time when he was contractually prohibited from recovering possession of the property.

   - The claim should be dismissed.

   (iii) DISCRETION OF THE COURT:

   - It is unclear (to me at least) if a Section 21 Notice requiring possession within the contractual term (without a break clause) is in fact invalid for the purposes of possession proceedings at such a time as the fixed term has subsequently (by the time of the hearing) come to an end.

This situation is different from the other cases in this section because the notice is served entirely pursuant to the statute and not in any way pursuant to a break clause and so should be distinguished from the other cases in this section.

- If the court is not minded to dismiss the claim, then submit that there is an arguable defence and directions for a Defence to be filed must be made. It may in fact be most appropriate in view of the overriding objective that this be the outcome, given the uncertainty of the situation.

- What *is* clear is that if the hearing takes place on a date that is still within the contractual period then the court cannot order possession and the court has no discretion here (s21(1)(a) Housing Act 1988).

Section 21(1)(a) Housing Act 1988

[The court must be] satisfied—

(a) that the assured shorthold tenancy has come to an end and no further assured tenancy (whether shorthold or not) is for the time being in existence, other than an assured shorthold periodic tenancy (whether statutory or not)...

2. **<u>If in reliance on a break clause, did the Section 21 Notice require possession after the time permitted by the break clause?</u>**

   (i) Did the s21 Notice require possession after the time permitted by the break clause?

   (ii) If not, then DEFENCE:

   - The terms of the break clause cited have been breached.

   - The Section 21 notice, being served purportedly in accordance with the break clause (and failing in this regard) is invalid and cannot be relied on (Hankey v Clavering, Court of Appeal (1942), confirmed in Fawaz v Aylward, Court of Appeal (1996) and approved in Mannai Investment Co Ltd v Eagle Star Assurance, House of Lords (1997) (see authorities under (1) below).

   - It matters not if the date given was a mistake – even an obvious mistake (Cadby v Martinez, Court of the King's Bench (1840), relied on in Hankey v Clavering, Court of Appeal (1942), and approved in Mannai Investment Co Ltd v Eagle Star Assurance, House of Lords (1997)) (see authorities under (2) below).

   (iii) DISCRETION OF THE COURT:

   - None. Court has no discretion to dispense with service of a valid Section 21 notice.

(1)

<u>Hankey v Clavering, Court of Appeal (1942)</u>

LORD GREENE MR: "… the real point in this case [is] whether or not the notice was good notice, that is to say, whether it had the effect of terminating the lease on Dec. 25, 1941 [in accordance with the break clause]. Notices of this kind, given under powers in leases of this description, are documents of a technical nature, technical for this reason, that if they are in proper form they have of their own force without any assent by the recipient the effect of bringing the demise to an end… They are documents which must do the thing which the proviso in the lease says they are to do; they must on their face and on a fair and reasonable construction do what the lease says they are to do".

Fawaz v Aylward, Court of Appeal (1996)

LORD JUSTICE NOURSE: "As Lord Greene MR makes clear in Hankey v Clavering… the notice determining the tenancy must, on its face and on a fair and reasonable construction, do what the lease provides that it is to do".

[See also Mannai Investment Co Ltd v Eagle Star Assurance, House of Lords (1997) below].

(2)

Cadby v Martinez, Court of the King's Bench (1840)

[Allowing an appeal against a judgment that a break clause was effectively operated even though there was an error in the date that possession was required by, the appellate court finding that it is irrelevant that the recipient of the notice knew that the date given was merely an error].

LORD DENMAN CJ: "In [no case] has a proviso or covenant in a deed been held to be satisfied by a notice inconsistent with the terms of it… No authority is required for so plain a proposition".

Hankey v Clavering, Court of Appeal (1942)

LORD GREENE MR: "In the present case what the respondent purported to do by the notice on its face was to bring the lease to an end on Dec. 21, and if he had said: "I hereby by this this notice give you 6 months' notice to determine your lease on Dec. 21, 1941 [instead of Dec. 25, 1941]", he would have been attempting to do something which he had no power to do; and however much the recipient might guess, or however certain he might be, that this was a mere slip, it would not cure the defect because the document immediately it is despatched is a document which is incapable on its face of producing the necessary legal consequences... The authority for that proposition, I think, is Cadby v Martinez, a case of the highest authority in these matters".

Mannai Investment Co Ltd v Eagle Star Assurance, House of Lords (1997)

LORD GOFF OF CHIEVELEY: "At first sight it seems unreasonable that the notice should not have been effective [it was an obvious mistake]... But the difficulty in the way of adopting this approach is that, on the authorities, it is inconsistent with the agreement of the parties as expressed in the clause... [on considering the authorities, including Cadby and Hankey] The principle is therefore clear. The agreement between the parties provides what notice has to be given to be effective to achieve the relevant result. The question in each case is: does the notice which was given, properly construed, comply with the agreed specification? If it does, it is effective for its purpose. If it does not, it is not so effective; and the mere fact that the person serving the notice plainly intended, and was trying, to give an effective notice under the clause, and that the recipient of the notice realised that he was doing so, makes no difference. This is because the notice, properly construed, did not comply with the agreement between the parties. The key does not fit the lock, and so the door will not open".

LORD JAUNCEY OF TULLICHETTLE: "Hankey v Clavering is a case of considerable authority, which has stood unchallenged and been applied for more than 50 years... I am not persuaded that there is any good reason for departing from the principles enunciated by Lord Greene MR".

3. **If in reliance on a break clause, does the clause expressly state that the landlord may rely upon it?**

   (i) Is the clause explicit about stating that the landlord can rely on it?

   (ii) If not, then DEFENCE:

   - If the clause is silent as to who may exercise it, then it must be interpreted as a tenant-only break clause (Dann v Spurrier, Court of Common Pleas (1803)).

   - If the clause states that only the tenant may use it, then it is of course a tenant-only break clause.

   (iii) DISCRETION OF THE COURT:

   - None – the court must proceed on the basis that there is no break clause (the Court of Common Pleas provides binding authority).

Dann v Spurrier, Court of Common Pleas (1803)

[Note: a (bona fide) 6-month break clause on a 12-month contract (for example) may be viewed as a contract for "6 or 12 months". If this view is not taken then it would be possible to distinguish Dann v Spurrier from break clauses].

Purported break clause: "London, 14th October 1791. Memorandum. I William Atkinson of Saint Olaves, Southwark [the initial tenant], have this day agreed to take on lease of John Spurrier [the landlord] the dwelling-house and premises now occupied by him in Old Broad-street, together with a bed-room… to hold for 7, 14, or 21 years, at the yearly rent of…"

[The lease was subsequently assigned to Richard Dann (the tenant) who took possession and paid the rent].

The landlord gave notice to quit at the 7-year mark; the tenant refused to leave and the landlord commenced an action for ejectment, and the tenant defended by filing a bill for specific performance of the contract.

LORD ALVANLEY: "In the Bishop Bath's case, it was resolved that the construction of law as to the commencement of leases should be taken strongest against the lessor, and most beneficially for the lessee. Another strong authority to this effect is Sir Rowland Heywood's case... If then, the principle be just, that a lease is to be construed most favourably for the lessee, why are we to determine in this instance that the option is in the lessor? If indeed a provision had been inserted that the lease should be determinable at the option of either party, the lessor would have been entitled to take advantage of it; but where no such proviso is inserted, the true construction seems to be that the lessee is entitled, at his option, to take that term which is most beneficial to himself... We think that where no custom of the country exists upon the subject, the principle of construing deeds between lessor and lessee requires us to hold, that where a grant is made in an alternative which cannot be determined by extrinsic circumstances, the option is left in the lessee. And we shall certify accordingly".

4. **If in reliance on a break clause, is the clause valid in contract law?**

   (i) Are the landlord's rights vis a vis the break clause mirrored by equivalent rights given to the tenant?

   (ii) If not, then DEFENCE:

   - Consumer protection legislation applies to tenancy agreements – the tenant is the consumer and the landlord is the provider of goods in the course of a business (London Borough of Newham v Khatun & others, Court of Appeal (2004)).

   - This clause is an unfair term creating a "significant imbalance in the parties' rights and obligations arising under the contract, to the detriment of the consumer":

Tenancies commencing before 1 October 2015	Reg. 5(1) The Unfair Terms in Consumer Contracts Regulations 1999
Tenancies commencing on or after 1 October 2015	s62(6) Consumer Rights Act 2015

   - As such it is not binding on the consumer:

Tenancies commencing before 1 October 2015	Reg. 8(1) The Unfair Terms in Consumer Contracts Regulations 1999
Tenancies commencing on or after 1 October 2015	s62(2) Consumer Rights Act 2015

   (iii) DISCRETION OF THE COURT:

   - If the court is persuaded that the clause is unfair then it has no discretion and must proceed as though there were no break clause.

London Borough of Newham v Khatun & others, Court of Appeal (2004)

LORD JUSTICE LAWS: "The question was whether the Unfair Terms in Consumer Contracts Regulations 1999 ("the Regulations") and Council Directive 93/13/EEC ("the Directive") applied to... contracts for the grant or transfer of an interest in land... In my judgment... the Directive and the Regulations apply to contracts relating to land".

Reg. 5(1) The Unfair Terms in Consumer Contracts Regulations 1999

A contractual term which has not been individually negotiated shall be regarded as unfair if, contrary to the requirement of good faith, it causes a significant imbalance in the parties' rights and obligations arising under the contract, to the detriment of the consumer.

Reg. 8(1) The Unfair Terms in Consumer Contracts Regulations 1999

An unfair term in a contract concluded with a consumer by a seller or supplier shall not be binding on the consumer.

s62 Consumer Rights Act 2015

...

(2) An unfair consumer notice is not binding on the consumer.

...

(6) A notice is unfair if, contrary to the requirement of good faith, it causes a significant imbalance in the parties' rights and obligations to the detriment of the consumer.

5. **Is the "break clause" actually a break clause?**

(i) If the clause requires the consent or agreement between the parties then it is not a break clause at all.

(ii) If so, then DEFENCE:

- This clause does not amount to a break clause as it cannot be unilaterally exercised. The wording of this clause requires consent or agreement – the tenant does not consent and does not agree. In earlier caselaw, one similar clause which was found could not be relied on as a break clause read: "[The property is hereby demised] for the term of twenty-one years, determinable, nonetheless, at the expiration of seven or fourteen years, if the said parties hereto shall so think fit" (Fowell v Tranter, Court of Exchequer (1864)).

- This clause is therefore no break clause at all.

(iii) DISCRETION OF THE COURT:

- If the court is persuaded that the clause is similar to that in Fowell v Tranter (1863), then the court must conclude that it is not a break clause and must proceed on the basis that there is no break clause (the Court of Exchequer is binding authority).

Fowell v Tranter, Court of Exchequer (1864)

Purported break clause: "[The property is hereby demised] for the term of twenty-one years, determinable, nonetheless, at the expiration of seven or fourteen years, if the said parties hereto shall so think fit".

HAYES, Serjt [counsel for the Defendant] successfully submitted that "grammatically, these words have but one meaning; the plural number should not have been used if the intention was that one of the parties might determine the lease without the other party's assent".

BRAMWELL, B: "The golden rule of construction is, that words are to be construed according to their natural meaning… The words naturally import that the joint assent of lessor and lessee shall be necessary to the determination of the lease".

PIGOTT, B: I think we are bound to carry out the contract which the parties have expressed, without speculating as to their intentions. The plaintiff's construction of the clause requires the word "respectively" to be introduced; the parties having left that word out, we cannot introduce it".

THE HOW TO RENT GUIDE

1. Has the correct version of the How to Rent Guide been served at the same time as or prior to the service of the Section 21 Notice?

N.B. If the most recent contractual AST commenced before 1 October 2015, this is not a requirement (Reg. 1(3) and (4) of the Assured Shorthold Tenancy Notices and Prescribed Requirements (England) Regulations 2015).

N.B. 2. This is also not a requirement for Registered Providers of Social Housing (Reg. 3(5)(a) of the Assured Shorthold Tenancy Notices and Prescribed Requirements (England) Regulations 2015).

(i) [refer to (i) in the diagram below] Was the How to Rent Guide served with the Section 21 Notice, and was the guide the most up-to-date version at the time of service?

OR

(ii) [refer to (ii) in the diagram below] Was the How to Rent Guide served at any time during the most recent replacement tenancy, and was the guide the most up-to-date version at the time of service?

OR

(iii) [refer to (iii) in the diagram below] Was the How to Rent Guide served at any time during the tenancy, was the guide the most up-to-date version at the time of service, and was that guide still the most up-to-date version at the time of the commencement of the most recent replacement tenancy?

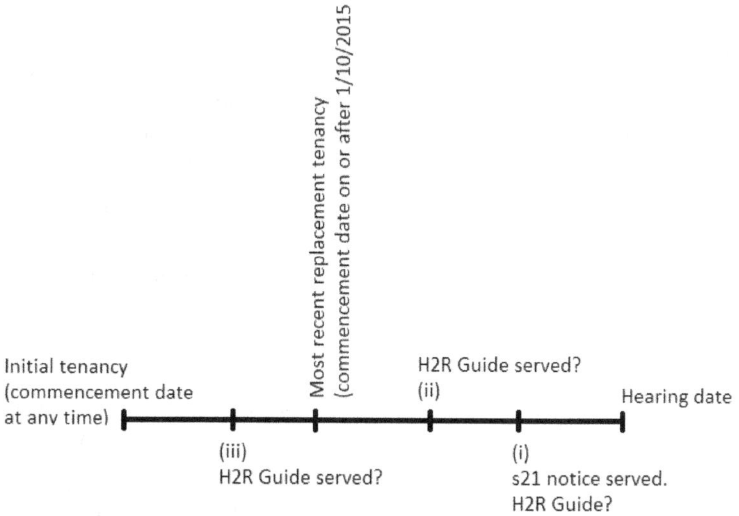

H2R GUIDE VERSIONS

VERSION	CHANGES	DESCRIPTION OF FRONT COVER
1 October 2015	Updated guidance.	Red brick wall with a blue front door. Turquoise box with text: "How to rent [tick box] The checklist for renting in England". White box with text: "This information is frequently updated. Search on GOV.UK for How to rent". Labelled "October 2015" in the white box. DCLG logo in the bottom right corner.

1 February 2016	Updated guidance.	Red brick wall with a blue front door. Turquoise box with text: "How to rent [tick box] The checklist for renting in England". White box with text: "This information is frequently updated. Search on GOV.UK for How to rent [//] The online version contains links you can click on to get more information. If you do not have internet access, ask your local library to help". Labelled "February 2016" in the white box. DCLG logo in the bottom right corner.
17 January 2018	Updated guidance.	Red brick wall with a blue front door. Turquoise box with text: "How to rent [tick box] The checklist for renting in England". White box with text: "This information is frequently updated. Search on GOV.UK for How to rent [//] The online version contains links you can click on to get more information. If you do not have internet access, ask your local library to help". Labelled "January 2018" in the white box. Ministry of Housing, Communities & Local Government logo in the bottom right corner.

26 June 2018	Title changed to "How to rent: A guide for current and prospective tenants in the private rented sector in England". This version also has an error regarding electrical safety inspections (states that the LL *must* provide a copy of any such inspection, on page 6). This version is also undated.	White background with a turquoise floor and a turquoise [for-sale-type] sign in the middle, with a peaked top side and a white banner at the top tracing the peak. A number of silhouetted figures of people apparently looking up at the sign in awe. Written in the sign: "HOW TO… RENT [//] A guide for current and prospective tenants in the private rented sector in England". States in bottom left: "Part of the How to Guides series". HM Government logo in the bottom right corner.
6 July 2018	Title reverted to "How to rent: the checklist for renting in England". This version also corrected the error on page 6.	White background with a turquoise floor and a turquoise [for-sale-type] sign in the middle, with a peaked top side and a white banner at the top tracing the peak. A number of silhouetted figures of people apparently looking up at the sign in awe. Written in the sign: "HOW TO… RENT [//] The checklist for renting in England". States in bottom left: "Part of the How to Guides series". HM Government logo in the bottom right corner.
31 May 2019	Updated guidance.	As above.

3 June 2019	The 3 June 2019 version is an update to the 31 May 2019 version on page 5 such that: *Corrected to reflect the rebranding of National Approved Letting Scheme (NALS) to Safeagent, and to update links to the GOV.UK client money protection scheme webpage.*	As above.
29 July 2019	The 29 July 2019 version is a further update to the 31 May 2019 version on page 4 such that: *The 'Before you start' section was updated to clarify Shelter's advisory role. The sentence 'If you don't have a guarantor, you can ask Shelter for help' was amended to 'If you don't have a guarantor, you can ask Shelter for advice'.*	As above.
10 December 2020	Updated guidance. Also note that the colour of the turquoise is slightly darker (this is not a submission – I mention it only to assist with quick identification!)	As above, but with a slightly darker shade of turquoise.

21 July 2021	This saw the addition of an easy read version. The standard version is exactly the same as of 10 December 2020. The Government webpage states: *How to Rent: easy read is produced to support tenants with learning disabilities. It is supplementary to How to Rent: the checklist for renting in England and is available as an additional supporting resource where appropriate.* *The easy read version helps people with learning disabilities to understand:* - *their rights and responsibilities when renting in the private rented sector* - *what to expect from a landlord before, during and after a tenancy* - *how to access support if anything goes wrong*	As above. EASY READ VERSION: White background for the top three-fifths, with a coloured drawing of a house to the (background) left and a drawing of a man standing in a blue suit checking a piece of paper to the (foreground) left with a man in a wheelchair in an orange jumper and blue trousers in the (foreground) centre. On the (middle-ground) right a depiction of a piece of paper labelled "Checklist" with a list of 4 (checked) tick boxes and a representation of writing next to each. Turquoise banner on the bottom two-fifths, with white writing: "How to rent [//] The checklist for renting in England" and then at the bottom left a small drawing of a man reading a white piece of paper containing an indistinguishable list, giving an enthusiastic thumbs up to the reader, next to which drawing are the words "Easy Read version".

(ii) If NO to ALL of (i), (ii), and (iii) above, then DEFENCE:

- A s21 notice "may not be given" at such time as a landlord has not provided prescribed information required by any regulations made pursuant to s21B(1) Housing Act 1988 (s21B(3) Housing Act 1988).

- The prescribed information is "the version of the document entitled "How to rent: the checklist for renting in England", as published by the Department for Communities and Local Government, that has effect for the time being" (Reg. 3(1) and (2) of the Assured Shorthold Tenancy Notices and Prescribed Requirements (England) Regulations 2015).

- The How to Rent Guide has not been served / has not been served so as to satisfy the Regulations:

  (i) No How to Rent Guide was served at any point (contrary to Reg. 3(1) and (2) of the Assured Shorthold Tenancy Notices and Prescribed Requirements (England) Regulations 2015);

  OR

  (ii) The H2R Guide that was served was not the most up-to-date version at the time of service (contrary to Reg. 3(1) and (2) of the Assured Shorthold Tenancy Notices and Prescribed Requirements (England) Regulations 2015);

  OR

  (iii) A H2R Guide was previously served, and although it was the most up-to-date version at that time there is a replacement tenancy which commenced at a time when a newer version of the H2R Guide was in force, which triggers a need for the Regulations to be complied with again (Reg. 3(5)(b) of the Assured Shorthold Tenancy Notices and Prescribed Requirements (England) Regulations 2015).

- The Section 21 notice is therefore invalid.

- The claim must therefore be dismissed.

(iii) DISCRETION OF THE COURT:

- None – mandatory wording – a s21 notice "may not be given".
- No discretion to dispense with service of a s21 notice.

<u>Section 21B Housing Act 1988</u>

(1) The Secretary of State may by regulations require information about the rights and responsibilities of a landlord and a tenant under an assured shorthold tenancy of a dwelling-house in England (or any related matters) to be given by a landlord under such a tenancy, or a person acting on behalf of such a landlord, to the tenant under such a tenancy.

...

(3) A notice under subsection (1) or (4) of section 21 may not be given in relation to an assured shorthold tenancy of a dwelling-house in England at a time when the landlord is in breach of a requirement imposed by regulations under subsection (1).

<u>Regulation 3 of the Assured Shorthold Tenancy Notices and Prescribed Requirements (England) Regulations 2015</u>

(1) A landlord under an assured shorthold tenancy of a dwelling-house in England, or a person acting on behalf of such a landlord, must give the tenant under that tenancy the information mentioned in paragraph (2).

(2) The information is the version of the document entitled "How to rent: the checklist for renting in England", as published by the Department for Communities and Local Government, that has effect for the time being.

...

(5) This regulation does not apply—

(a) where the landlord is a private registered provider of social housing; or

(b) where—

(i) the tenancy ("the new tenancy") is a replacement tenancy;

(ii) the landlord, or a person acting on behalf of the landlord, provided the tenant with the document mentioned in paragraph (2) under an earlier tenancy; and

(iii) the version of the document provided to the tenant under the earlier tenancy is the same version as the version which is in effect on the first day of the new tenancy.

Regulation 1 of the Assured Shorthold Tenancy Notices and Prescribed Requirements (England) Regulations 2015

...

(3) Subject to paragraph (4), these Regulations apply in relation to an assured shorthold tenancy of a dwelling-house in England granted on or after 1st October 2015.

(4) These Regulations do not apply to an assured shorthold tenancy that came into being under section 5(2) of the Housing Act 1988 on or after 1st October 2015 on the coming to an end of an assured shorthold tenancy that was granted before that date [i.e. a periodic tenancy arising where the most recent written tenancy was granted before 1 October 2015].

2. **<u>Is the Claimant relying on service of the 26 June 2018 version?</u>**

(i) Is the Claimant relying on service of the 26 June 2018 version?

(ii) If yes, then DEFENCE:

- The Regulations require service of "the version of the document entitled "How to rent: the checklist for renting in England", as published by the Department for Communities and Local Government, that has effect for the time being" (Reg. 3(1) and (2) of the Assured Shorthold Tenancy Notices and Prescribed Requirements (England) Regulations 2015).

- This document is not that document. Instead it is a document entitled "How to rent: A guide for current and prospective tenants in the private rented sector in England".

- The Regulations are prescriptive. The proper guide has not been served. The courts should apply the literal rule of interpretation, especially where there is no ambiguity in the wording of the legislation (Express Newspapers Ltd. V Macshane, House of Lords (1980)).

- The s21 notice is therefore invalid and the claim must be dismissed.

(iii) DISCRETION OF THE COURT:

- The court may not be persuaded to dismiss the claim on the basis of the above. The Government webpage is clear that it sets out "the most up to date version of the Guide… incorporat[ing] all changes detailed in the update history below", in which list the 26 June 2018 version is included. Even using the literal rule of interpretation, the court may therefore consider that the document "How to rent: A guide for current and prospective tenants in the private rented sector in England" is indeed a <u>version</u> of the document "How to rent: the checklist for renting in England" – after all, the Regulation does not state that the document always needs to be called the same thing, and even in this guide I am referring to it as "the 26 June 2018 version". The Oxford English Dictionary defines "version" as "a form of something that is slightly different from an earlier form or from other forms of the same thing". This could count. Even if it does not, the court may instead consider that the mischief rule is a more appropriate interpretative basis for answering this question.

- If the court is not persuaded to dismiss the claim on the basis of these submissions, you should respectfully ask the court to make directions for a Defence.

Regulation 3 of the Assured Shorthold Tenancy Notices and Prescribed Requirements (England) Regulations 2015

(1) A landlord under an assured shorthold tenancy of a dwelling-house in England, or a person acting on behalf of such a landlord, must give the tenant under that tenancy the information mentioned in paragraph (2).

(2) The information is the version of the document entitled "How to rent: the checklist for renting in England", as published by the Department for Communities and Local Government, that has effect for the time being.

Express Newspapers Ltd. V Macshane, House of Lords (1980)

LORD DIPLOCK: "It is not for the judge to invent fancied ambiguities as an excuse for failing to give effect to [legislation's] plain meaning because they themselves consider that the consequences of doing so would be inexpedient, or even unjust or immoral".

3. Is the Claimant relying on service of the 21 July 2021 version?

(i) If the Claimant is relying on service of the 21 July 2021 version, have they also served the "easy read" version alongside the standard version?

(ii) If not, then DEFENCE:

- The Government webpage is clear that it sets out "the most up to date version of the Guide" and it includes the "easy read" version alongside the standard version.

- On page 23 of the "easy read" guide, it states: "Papers the landlord MUST give you", and in the subsequent list it includes as the first item: "A printed copy of this How to Rent Guide". This is written alongside a picture of the front cover of the "easy read" version (see above for a description of the front cover).

- The claimant has not served this document and has therefore not served *the* version which has effect for the time being, which currently consists of two iterations (standard and easy read), both of which must be served.

- NOTE: The above argument may be difficult to run for a number of reasons. However, if the Defendant has learning difficulties then it is clear that the easy read version is intended to assist such a Defendant understand their rights and how to access support. It would be more persuasive to run this argument for such a Defendant, and in such a case it may also be possible to raise public law defences as well.

(iii) DISCRETION OF THE COURT:

- If the court is persuaded that both the standard version and the easy read version should have been served together then there is no discretion as the s21 notice will be invalid.

4. **Was the How to Rent Guide served as a hard copy?**

(i) Was the How to Rent Guide (if served) served as a hard copy, or if by email did the Defendant give prior authority (for example in the tenancy agreement) for documents to be served by email and to the email address used?

(ii) If not, then DEFENCE:

- Service in hard copy is a requirement (Reg. 3(3)(a) Assured Shorthold Tenancy Notices and Prescribed Requirements (England) Regulations 2015).
- Only if the tenant has given an email address for service may the H2R Guide be served by email (Reg. 3(3)(b)).
- This is a closed list – no other method of service is permitted.
- There has therefore been a failure of service and the prescribed information has not been served.
- The s21 notice is therefore invalid and the claim must be dismissed.

(iii) DISCRETION OF THE COURT:

- None – the s21 is invalid and the court has no discretion to dispense with service of a s21 notice.

Regulation 3(3) Assured Shorthold Tenancy Notices and Prescribed Requirements (England) Regulations 2015

The information may be provided to the tenant—

(a) in hard copy; or

(b) where the tenant has notified the landlord, or a person acting on behalf of the landlord, of an e-mail address at which the tenant is content to accept service of notices and other documents given under or in connection with the tenancy, by e-mail.

GAS SAFETY RECORD

1. **Where there is a gas fitting in the demised premises, has the relevant Gas Safety Record been provided in full?**

N.B. If the most recent contractual AST commenced before 1 October 2015, this is not a requirement for the purposes of s21 validity (Reg. 1(3) and (4) Assured Shorthold Tenancy Notices and Prescribed Requirements (England) Regulations 2015, Minister v Hathaway & Hathaway, Court of Appeal (2021)).

(i) If there is a gas fitting in the demised premises, was there a Gas Safety Record available for the property at the start of the tenancy, and has this been provided to the tenant at the same time as or prior to the service of the Section 21 Notice, and has any subsequent GSR produced likewise been provided to the tenant at the same time as or prior to the service of the Section 21 Notice?

(ii) Does the Record provided constitute a FULL Gas Safety Record?

The Elements of a Full Gas Safety Record

(i)	Date of inspection
(ii)	Address of property
(iii)	Name and address of landlord (or agent)
(iv)	Description and location of each appliance or flue checked (EVERY appliance or flue checked?)
(v)	Defects identified
(vi)	Any remedial action taken

(vii)	If work was carried out, then confirmation that following this work the following was immediately checked and any follow-up defects reported to the landlord or agent: ▪ Effectiveness of any connected flue ▪ Supply of combustion air ▪ Operating pressure or heat input ▪ The appliance's safe functioning
(viii)	Name and signature of the engineer carrying out the inspection
(ix)	Registration number of the engineer or his employer

(iii) If not, then DEFENCE:

- It is a prescribed requirement that the Gas Safety Record that relates to the beginning of the tenancy and any subsequent GSR has been given to the tenant (Reg. 2 para. 1(b) of the Assured Shorthold Tenancy Notices and Prescribed Requirements (England) Regulations 2015) (Reg. 36 para. 6 of the Gas Safety (Installation and Use) Regulations 1998) (Trecarrell v Rouncefield, Court of Appeal (2020));

- The Gas Safety Record must contain all the information above (Reg. 36 paras. 6(a) and 3(c) of the Gas Safety (Installation and Use) Regulations 1998);

- Non-compliance makes the notice invalid (s21A(1) Housing Act 1988).

(iv) DISCRETION OF THE COURT:

- None. A notice "may not be given" (mandatory wording) while in breach of a prescribed requirement (s21A(1) Housing Act 1988)

Reg. 1 Assured Shorthold Tenancy Notices and Prescribed Requirements (England) Regulations 2015

...

(3) Subject to paragraph (4), these Regulations apply in relation to an assured shorthold tenancy of a dwelling-house in England granted on or after 1st October 2015.

(4) These Regulations do not apply to an assured shorthold tenancy that came into being under section 5(2) of the Housing Act 1988 [a statutory periodic tenancy] on or after 1st October 2015 on the coming to an end of an assured shorthold tenancy that was granted before that date.

Section 21A(1) Housing Act 1988

A notice under subsection (1) or (4) of section 21 may not be given in relation to an assured shorthold tenancy of a dwelling-house in England at a time when the landlord is in breach of a prescribed requirement.

Regulation 2 paragraph 1(b) of the Assured Shorthold Tenancy Notices and Prescribed Requirements (England) Regulations 2015

... the requirements prescribed for the purposes of section 21A of the Act are the requirements contained in... [among others] paragraph (6) or (as the case may be) paragraph (7) [where there is no relevant gas fitting in the demised premises] of regulation 36 of the Gas Safety (Installation and Use) Regulations 1998 (requirement to provide tenant with a gas safety certificate).

Regulation 26 of the Gas Safety (Installation and Use) Regulations 1998

...

(9) Where a person performs work on a gas appliance he shall immediately thereafter examine—

(a) the effectiveness of any flue;

(b) the supply of combustion air;

(c) its operating pressure or heat input or, where necessary, both;

(d) its operation so as to ensure its safe functioning,

and forthwith take all reasonable practicable steps to notify any defect to the responsible person and, where different, the owner of the premises in which the appliance is situated or, where neither is reasonably practicable, in the case of an appliance supplied with liquefied petroleum gas, the supplier of gas to the appliance, or, in any other case, the transporter.

Regulation 36 of the Gas Safety (Installation and Use) Regulations 1998

...

(3) ... a landlord shall—

...

(c) ensure that a record in respect of any appliance or flue so checked is made and retained for a period of 2 years from the date of that check, which record shall include the following information—

(i) the date on which the appliance or flue was checked;

(ii) the address of the premises at which the appliance or flue is installed;

(iii) the name and address of the landlord of the premises (or, where appropriate, his agent) at which the appliance or flue is installed;

(iv) a description of and the location of each appliance or flue checked;

(v) any defect identified;

(vi) any remedial action taken;

(vii) confirmation that the check undertaken complies with the requirements of paragraph (9) below;

(viii) the name and signature of the individual carrying out the check; and

(ix) the registration number with which that individual, or his employer, is registered with a body approved by the Executive for the purposes of regulation 3(3) of these Regulations.

...

(6) ... every landlord shall ensure that—

(a) a copy of the record made pursuant to the requirements of paragraph (3)(c) above is given to each existing tenant of [the] premises... ; and

(b) a copy of the last record made in respect of each appliance or flue is given to any new tenant of premises to which the record relates...

...

(9) A safety check carried out pursuant to paragraph (3) above shall include, but shall not be limited to, an examination of the matters referred to in sub-paragraphs (a) to (d) of regulation 26(9) of these Regulations.

Minister v Hathaway & Hathaway, Court of Appeal (2021)

[Although directly dealing with the provision of an EPC certificate, the issue actually considered was adherence with the prescribed requirements of s21A(1) Housing Act 1988, which includes the Gas Safety Record].

LORD JUSTICE ARNOLD: "The landlords contend that this requirement did not apply because the tenant's tenancy of the flat was not "an assured shorthold tenancy of a dwelling house in England granted on or after 1 October 2015... I agree with HHJ Simpkiss that the landlords are correct".

Trecarrell v Rouncefield, Court of Appeal (2020)

LORD JUSTICE PATTEN: "The effect of regulation 2(2) is to remove the 28-day time limit in paragraph (6)(a) and also… the requirement in paragraph (6)(b) that a new tenant should be supplied with a copy of the current GSR prior to taking up occupation… The landlord has no obligation to provide the GSR prior to granting the tenancy. The right of the tenant to see the GSR arises only once he or she has become the tenant of the premises".

"I am not persuaded that a failure to carry out the next safety check within 12 months of the last one means that the landlord cannot comply with paragraph 6(a) as a prescribed requirement if he serves the tenant with a copy of the record once the check has been carried out".

"The outcome of the appeal therefore depends, in my view, on whether the February 2018 GSR [not the GSR that covered the beginning of the tenancy, but a subsequent GSR] was given to Ms Rouncefield later than when she was served with the s21 notice. If she received it before or with the s21 notice then the claimant's appeal must be allowed. If she received it after service of the s21 notice then the appeal must be dismissed for that reason alone".

LADY JUSTICE KING: "For my part I agree with Patten LJ that the features he has identified in his judgment serve to support an interpretation that failure to provide a GSR by a landlord, either at the beginning of a tenancy or following a subsequent annual safety inspection, is not fatal to his ability to give notice under s21 providing that the relevant certificate has been provided before service of the notice".

2. **Where there is no relevant gas fitting in the demised premises, but there is nonetheless a gas supply to the property (e.g. hot water provided to the demised premises via a gas boiler), has the relevant Gas Safety Record been provided in full, OR has a copy of that Record been displayed prominently in the premises WITH a written statement that the tenant is entitled to his own copy of the same, WITH an address to which the tenant can write to the landlord to ask for his own copy?**

N.B. If the most recent contractual AST commenced before 1 October 2015, this is not a requirement for the purposes of s21 validity (Reg. 1(3) and (4) Assured Shorthold Tenancy Notices and Prescribed Requirements (England) Regulations 2015, Minister v Hathaway & Hathaway, Court of Appeal (2021)) (see above).

(i) Where there is no relevant gas fitting in the demised premises, but still a gas supply, has the Record (relating to the beginning of the tenancy AND any subsequent GSRs) been provided with or prior to, or displayed prominently (with the statement as above) prior to, the service of the Section 21 Notice?

(ii) If not, then DEFENCE:

- It is a prescribed requirement where there is no relevant gas fitting in the demised premises (but still a gas supply) that the Gas Safety Record that relates to the beginning of the tenancy AND any subsequent GSRs has either been given to the tenant OR has been displayed in a prominent position with the statement as above (Reg. 36 para. 7 of the Gas Safety (Installation and Use) Regulations 1998);

- The Record must contain all the information as above;

- Non-compliance makes the s21 notice invalid (s21A(1) Housing Act 1988).

(iii) DISCRETION OF THE COURT:

- None. A notice "may not be given" (mandatory wording) while in breach of a prescribed requirement (s21A(1) Housing Act 1988)

See above, but also in particular:

Section 21A(1) Housing Act 1988

A notice under subsection (1) or (4) of section 21 may not be given in relation to an assured shorthold tenancy of a dwelling-house in England at a time when the landlord is in breach of a prescribed requirement.

Regulation 2 paragraph 1(b) of the Assured Shorthold Tenancy Notices and Prescribed Requirements (England) Regulations 2015

... the requirements prescribed for the purposes of section 21A of the Act are the requirements contained in... paragraph (6) or (as the case may be) paragraph (7) of regulation 36 of the Gas Safety (Installation and Use) Regulations 1998 (requirement to provide tenant with a gas safety certificate).

Regulation 36 of the Gas Safety (Installation and Use) Regulations 1998

...

(7) Where there is no relevant gas appliance in any room occupied or to be occupied by the tenant in relevant premises, the landlord may, instead of ensuring that a copy of the record referred to in paragraph (6) above is given to the tenant, ensure that there is displayed in a prominent position in the premises... a copy of the record with a statement endorsed on it that the tenant is entitled to have his own copy of the record on request to the landlord at an address specified in the statement; and on any such request being made, the landlord shall give to the tenant a copy of the record as soon as is practicable.

ENERGY PERFORMANCE CERTIFICATE

1. Has the Energy Performance Certificate been provided?

N.B. If the most recent contractual AST commenced before 1 October 2015, this is not a requirement (Reg. 1(3) and (4) Assured Shorthold Tenancy Notices and Prescribed Requirements (England) Regulations 2015, Minister v Hathaway & Hathaway, Court of Appeal (2021)).

(i) Was the EPC for the Property served at the same time as or prior to the service of the Section 21 Notice, and was it valid at the time it was given?

(ii) If not, then DEFENCE:

- A s21 notice "may not be given" at a time when the LL has not provided an EPC (s21A(1) HA 1988; Reg. 2(1)(a) Assured Shorthold Tenancy Notices and Prescribed Requirements (England) Regulations 2015; Reg. 6(5) Energy Performance of Buildings (England and Wales) Regulations 2012).

- For compliance, the EPC must be valid at the time of service (Reg. 6(5) Energy Performance of Buildings (England and Wales) Regulations 2012)).

- An EPC was not served, or it was not valid when it was served, and therefore the s21 notice cannot be valid.

- These proceedings must therefore be dismissed.

(iii) DISCRETION OF THE COURT:

- None. A notice "may not be given" (mandatory wording) while in breach of a prescribed requirement (s21A(1) Housing Act 1988).

[NOTE – it is unclear whether the EPC needs to be valid <u>at the date of service of the Section 21 notice</u>. I suspect that it does not, but there is no case law and if it is not valid at that time then this may be a point worth raising in the defence. See the introductory discussion chapter on Gas Safety Certificate for a similar, though clearly distinguishable, situation.

NOTE ALSO – it is not clear whether a property needs to have actually passed the EPC inspection in order for the certificate to be "valid". Is a certificate which records that the property failed an inspection, valid? I suspect that it is valid, but as far as I am aware this is not a definition which has been considered by the courts.]

Reg. 1 Assured Shorthold Tenancy Notices and Prescribed Requirements (England) Regulations 2015

…

(3) Subject to paragraph (4), these Regulations apply in relation to an assured shorthold tenancy of a dwelling-house in England granted on or after 1st October 2015.

(4) These Regulations do not apply to an assured shorthold tenancy that came into being under section 5(2) of the Housing Act 1988 [a statutory periodic tenancy] on or after 1st October 2015 on the coming to an end of an assured shorthold tenancy that was granted before that date.

Minister v Hathaway & Hathaway, Court of Appeal (2021)

LORD JUSTICE ARNOLD: "The landlords contend that this requirement did not apply because the tenant's tenancy of the flat was not "an assured shorthold tenancy of a dwelling house in England granted on or after 1 October 2015… I agree with HHJ Simpkiss that the landlords are correct".

Section 21A(1) Housing Act 1988

A notice under subsection (1) or (4) of section 21 may not be given in relation to an assured shorthold tenancy of a dwelling-house in England at a time when the landlord is in breach of a prescribed requirement.

Regulation 2 paragraph 1(a) of the Assured Shorthold Tenancy Notices and Prescribed Requirements (England) Regulations 2015

… the requirements prescribed for the purposes of section 21A of the Act are the requirements contained in… [among others] regulation 6(5) of the Energy Performance of Buildings (England and Wales) Regulations 2012 (requirement to provide an energy performance certificate to a tenant or buyer free of charge).

Reg. 6(5) Energy Performance of Buildings (England and Wales) Regulations 2012

The relevant person must ensure that a valid energy performance certificate has been given free of charge to the person who ultimately becomes the buyer or tenant.

DEPOSIT PROTECTION AND PRESCRIBED INFORMATION

1. **If a deposit was paid, was it protected in time OR was it returned to the tenant prior to service of the s21 notice?**

    (i) If a deposit was paid, was it protected in time (as below) OR was it returned to the tenant prior to the service of the s21 notice?

Deposit Protection Deadlines for the Purposes of Section 21 Validity

AST commenced	Deposit received by LL	Protection required by	Authority
Any time	On or after 6 April 2012	Within 30 days of receipt	213(3) Housing Act 2004 as amended by s184(2)(a) Localism Act 2011 amendment brought into force on 6 April 2012 by Art. 8(c) The Localism Act 2011 (Commencement No. 4 and Transitional, Transitory and Saving Provisions) Order 2012
Any time	Between 6 April 2007 and 5 April 2012 inclusive	<u>Before</u> 6 May 2012	Art. 16 The Localism Act 2011 (Commencement No. 4 and Transitional, Transitory and Saving Provisions) Order 2012
Before 6 April 2007 and becoming statutory periodic on or <u>after</u> 6 April 2007, such statutory periodic tenancy still being in existence on 26 March 2015	Before 6 April 2007	<u>Before</u> 24 June 2015	S215A(2) and s215A(3)(a) Housing Act 2004

Before 6 April 2007 and becoming statutory periodic <u>before</u> 6 April 2007, or any other situation not accounted for above	Before 6 April 2007	Any time prior to service of the s21 notice	S215(1) Housing Act 2004

It is always an alternative to return the deposit to the tenant prior to the service of the s21 notice (s215(2A)(a) Housing Act 2004).

In addition, if a s214(1) claim has already been determined in the courts / withdrawn / settled prior to service of the s21 notice, then breach of the requirements will not invalidate the s21 notice (s215(2A)(b) Housing Act 2004).

In addition, if the current tenancy is a replacement tenancy, and the deposit was protected late under the original tenancy, nonetheless – IF the deposit was protected AND the prescribed information was served AND the deposit continues to be held with that particular protection scheme – then the late protection of the deposit will not be a defence to the s21 notice (s215B(2) Housing Act 2004).

(ii) If not, then DEFENCE:

- "No s21 notice may be given" if the deposit is not protected (s215(1) Housing Act 2004) (subject to the exceptions set out above);
- In addition, "no s21 notice may be given" if the deposit was not protected in time (as per the deadlines above) (s215(1A) Housing Act 2004) (subject to the exceptions set out above);
- The deposit was not returned and the deposit was not protected / was not protected in time, therefore the s21 notice is invalid and the claim must be dismissed.

(iii) DISCRETION OF THE COURT:

- None – "no s21 notice may be given" (mandatory wording) when the deposit is not protected and / or was not protected in time. Cannot dispense with service of a s21 notice.

s213(3) Housing Act 2004

Where a landlord receives a tenancy deposit in connection with a shorthold tenancy, the initial requirements of an authorised scheme must be complied with by the landlord in relation to the deposit within the period of 30 days beginning with the date on which it is received.

s184(2)(a) Localism Act 2011

In section 213 (requirements relating to tenancy deposits)—

(a)in subsection (3) (landlord's requirement to comply with initial requirements within 14 days of receipt of deposit) for "14" substitute "30"...

Art. 8(c) The Localism Act 2011 (Commencement No. 4 and Transitional, Transitory and Saving Provisions) Order 2012

Subject to articles 9, 12, 13, 16, and 18 to 20, the following provisions of the Act (so far as they are not yet in force) come into force in relation to England and Wales on 6th April 2012—

...

(c) section 184

Art. 16 The Localism Act 2011 (Commencement No. 4 and Transitional, Transitory and Saving Provisions) Order 2012

(1) Subject to paragraph (2), the amendments made by section 184 of the Act apply in respect of any tenancy deposit received by a landlord in connection with a shorthold tenancy where the tenancy was in effect on or after 6th April 2012.

(2) Those amendments do not apply in respect of a tenancy deposit received by a landlord in connection with a shorthold tenancy where—

(a) the tenancy was in effect on or after 6th April 2012, and

(b) the landlord has, before the end of the period of 30 days beginning with that date—

(i) complied with the initial requirements of an authorised scheme in relation to the deposit, and

(ii) given to the tenant and any relevant person the information prescribed for the purposes of section 213(5) of the Housing Act 2004.

S215A Housing Act 2004

...

(2) If, on the commencement date—

(a) the periodic tenancy is in existence, and

(b) all or part of the deposit paid in connection with the fixed term tenancy continues to be held in connection with the periodic tenancy, section 213 applies in respect of the deposit that continues to be held in connection with the periodic tenancy, and any additional deposit held in connection with that tenancy, with the modifications set out in subsection (3).

(3) The modifications are that, instead of the things referred to in section 213(3) and (5) being required to be done within the time periods set out in section 213(3) and (6)(b), those things are required to be done—

(a) before the end of the period of 90 days beginning with the commencement date.

...

S215 Housing Act 2004

(1) Subject to subsection (2A), if (whether before, on or after 6 April 2007) a tenancy deposit has been paid in connection with a shorthold tenancy, no section 21 notice may be given in relation to the tenancy at a time when the deposit is not being held in accordance with an authorised scheme.

(1A) Subject to subsection (2A), if a tenancy deposit has been paid in connection with a shorthold tenancy on or after 6 April 2007, no section 21 notice may be given in relation to the tenancy at a time when section 213(3) has not been complied with in relation to the deposit.

...

(2A) Subsections (1) [and] (1A)... do not apply in a case where—

(a) the deposit has been returned to the tenant in full or with such deductions as are agreed between the landlord and tenant, or

(b) an application to the county court has been made under section 214(1) and has been determined by the court, withdrawn or settled by agreement between the parties.

...

Section 215B(2) Housing Act 2004

[Where Section 215B applies], "In their application to the new tenancy, the requirements of section 213(3) [is] treated as if [it] had been complied with by the landlord in relation to the deposit".

2. **Has the prescribed information been provided to the tenant and any relevant person in full in respect of deposit protection at the same time as or prior to service of the Section 21 notice?**

   (i) If a deposit was paid, and protected, was the prescribed information provided to the tenant and any relevant person (the person who paid the deposit) in full (as below) at the same time as or prior to service of the s21 notice, in the prescribed form or a form substantially to the same effect?

Prescribed Information Required in Full

(a) the name, address, telephone number, e-mail address and any fax number of the scheme administrator of the authorised tenancy deposit scheme applying to the deposit;

(b) any information contained in a leaflet supplied by the scheme administrator to the landlord which explains the operation of the provisions contained in sections 212 to 215 of, and Schedule 10 to, the Act;

(c) the procedures that apply under the scheme by which an amount in respect of a deposit may be paid or repaid to the tenant at the end of the shorthold tenancy ("the tenancy");

(d) the procedures that apply under the scheme where either the landlord or the tenant is not contactable at the end of the tenancy;

(e) the procedures that apply under the scheme where the landlord and the tenant dispute the amount to be paid or repaid to the tenant in respect of the deposit;

(f) the facilities available under the scheme for enabling a dispute relating to the deposit to be resolved without recourse to litigation; and

(g) the following information in connection with the tenancy in respect of which the deposit has been paid—

(i) the amount of the deposit paid;

(ii) the address of the property to which the tenancy relates;

(iii) the name, address, telephone number, and any e-mail address or fax number of the landlord;

(iv) the name, address, telephone number, and any e-mail address or fax number of the tenant, including such details that should be used by the landlord or scheme administrator for the purpose of contacting the tenant at the end of the tenancy;

(v) the name, address, telephone number and any e-mail address or fax number of any relevant person;

(vi) the circumstances when all or part of the deposit may be retained by the landlord, by reference to the terms of the tenancy; and

(vii) confirmation (in the form of a certificate signed by the landlord) that—

(aa) the information he provides under this sub-paragraph is accurate to the best of his knowledge and belief; and

(bb) he has given the tenant the opportunity to sign any document containing the information provided by the landlord under this article by way of confirmation that the information is accurate to the best of his knowledge and belief.

SOURCE: Article 2 of The Housing (Tenancy Deposits) (Prescribed Information) Order 2007.

This will usually require service of three things: 1. A signed certificate of protection; 2. A "prescribed information proforma from the deposit protection company; and 3. An "Information for Tenants" booklet and / or terms and conditions of the scheme.

It is always an alternative to return the deposit to the tenant prior to the service of the s21 notice (s215(2A)(a) Housing Act 2004).

In addition, if a s214(1) claim has already been determined in the courts / withdrawn / settled prior to service of the s21 notice, then breach of the requirements will not invalidate the s21 notice (s215(2A)(b) Housing Act 2004).

Service of part information within the tenancy agreement or even in a separate document is NOT SUFFICIENT ((1) Ayannuga v Swindells, Court of Appeal (2012).

It is INSUFFICIENT for the LL to state that the information was already well known to the tenant, or that the information was readily available (for example, online) ((2) Ayannuga v Swindells, Court of Appeal (2012)) (Kahlon v Isherwood, Court of Appeal (2011)).

(ii) If not, then DEFENCE:

- Service of the prescribed information is a prescribed requirement (s213(6)(a) Housing Act 2004);
- No Section 21 notice may be given until such time as the prescribed information has been served (subject to the exceptions above) (s215(2) Housing Act 2004);
- The Section 21 notice is therefore invalid.

(iii) DISCRETION OF THE COURT:

- If all the information has not been precisely provided, has it been provided in a form "substantially to the same effect"?
    - A matter of fact and degree ((3) Ayannuga v Swindells, Court of Appeal (2012));
    - Any information regarding the procedure for the resolution of disputes is certainly substantive ((4) Ayannuga v Swindells, Court of Appeal (2012));
    - It is substantially to the same effect for a certificate to be signed by an agent for the LL (and likewise it does not need to be signed in accordance with Section 44 Companies Act 2006 if the LL is a company (Northwood (Solihull) Ltd v Cooke Fearn and Others, Court of Appeal (2022)).
- If not, none – "no s21 notice may be given" (mandatory wording) until s213(6)(a) has been complied with. Cannot dispense with service of a s21 notice.

Section 213 Housing Act 2004

...

(5) A landlord who has received such a tenancy deposit must give the tenant and any relevant person such information relating to—

(a) the authorised scheme applying to the deposit,

(b) compliance by the landlord with the initial requirements of the scheme in relation to the deposit, and

(c) the operation of provisions of this Chapter in relation to the deposit, as may be prescribed.

...

(6) The information required by subsection (5) must be given to the tenant and any relevant person—

(a)in the prescribed form or in a form substantially to the same effect

...

Section 215 Housing Act 2004

...

(2) Subject to subsection (2A), if section 213(6) is not complied with in relation to a deposit given in connection with a shorthold tenancy, no section 21 notice may be given in relation to the tenancy until such time as section 213(6)(a) is complied with.

(2A) Subsection... (2) [does] not apply in a case where—

(a) the deposit has been returned to the tenant in full or with such deductions as are agreed between the landlord and tenant, or

(b) an application to the county court has been made under section 214(1) and has been determined by the court, withdrawn or settled by agreement between the parties.

Article 2 of The Housing (Tenancy Deposits) (Prescribed Information) Order 2007

(1) The following is prescribed information for the purposes of section 213(5) of the Housing Act 2004 ("the Act")—

[as per table above].

Ayannuga v Swindells, Court of Appeal (2012)

(1) LORD JUSTICE ETHERTON: "It is true that the Tenancy Agreement and the Additional Information Document addressed the procedure that was to apply if and when the tenancy came to an end and the deposit had to be returned… [However] they do not address… the procedural provisions in the scheme itself. […] I am quite satisfied that the only proper conclusion which could be reached in this case is that there was a failure by the Respondent substantially to comply with the statutory requirements in view of the entire omission of the information specified in each of paras 2(1)(c) to (f) of the Housing Order".

(2) LORD JUSTICE ETHERTON: "It is no answer for the Respondent to assert that the information could have been obtained by the Appellant making her own enquiries by means of the internet or telephoning the Respondent's agent or the scheme's administrator or in some other way. Section 213(5) of the 2004 Act requires the information to be provided by the landlord".

LORD JUSTICE LEWISON: "Mr Gibson-Lee [for the LL] submitted that the tenant had the means of obtaining the information even if it was not actually provided to her by the landlord. But the statutory requirement is that the landlord must provide the information… I am satisfied that the complete failure to engage with paras (e) and (f) and indeed paras (c) and (d) mean that the substance of the requirement to provide information was not complied with".

(3) LORD JUSTICE LEWISON: "We must compare the form or information prescribed on the one hand and the information in fact supplied on the other. We must then ask, in light of the purpose of the notice or the provision of the information, whether the substance of the information has been supplied bearing in mind that that is a matter of fact and degree".

(4) LORD JUSTICE LEWISON: "The purpose of a tenancy deposit scheme... is not merely the purpose of safeguarding tenancy deposits. There is also the purpose of facilitating the resolution of disputes... [A]n explanation of the procedure is of itself substantive".

Kahlon v Isherwood, Court of Appeal (2011)

LORD JUSTICE PATTEN: "Relevance or materiality has to be assessed by reference to the purpose of the notice. But where the provision in the prescribed form is clearly part of the substance of the notice as found in Manel v Memon it is no answer to its omission to say that the information it conveys was well known to the tenant at the relevant time".

Northwood (Solihull) Ltd v Cooke Fearn and Others, Court of Appeal (2022)

LORD JUSTICE LEWISON: "That Parliament did not consider that authentication by an agent was fatal to the validity of a certificate is, to my mind, [clear]... [T]he requirement to give the tenant "the prescribed information" was fully and precisely complied with... That information was authenticated on behalf of the landlord by someone authorised to do so. If an authorised and authenticated certificate, containing all the right information, is given to the tenant... I would hold that even if the certificate did not strictly comply with the requirements about authentication by the landlord, it was still valid".

IMPROVEMENT NOTICE FROM THE LOCAL AUTHORITY

1. **Was the landlord served with an improvement notice or a notice for emergency remedial action prior to the service of the Section 21 notice?**

   (i) Was the landlord served with a notice under Section 11, 12, or 40(7) Housing Act 2004, and was the Section 21 notice served within 6 months of that (or where the s11, 12, or 40(7) notice was suspended, within 6 months of the ending of the suspension)?

   (ii) If so, then DEFENCE:

   - Improvement notices under Section 11 or Section 12, and emergency remedial action notices under Section 40(7) Housing Act 2007, are "relevant notices" for the purposes of Section 21 validity (s33(13) Deregulation Act 2015);

   - No Section 21 notice may be served within 6 months of service of a relevant notice, or within 6 months of the lifting of a suspension of such a notice (whichever the case may be) (s33(1) Deregulation Act 2015);

   - The Section 21 notice is therefore invalid.

(iii) DISCRETION OF THE COURT:

   - None – "a section 21 notice may not be given" (mandatory wording). Cannot dispense with service of a s21 notice.

Section 33(1) Deregulation Act 2015

Where a relevant notice is served in relation to a dwelling-house in England, a section 21 notice may not be given in relation to an assured shorthold tenancy of the dwelling-house—

(a) within six months beginning with the day of service of the relevant notice, or

(b) where the operation of the relevant notice has been suspended, within six months beginning with the day on which the suspension ends.

Section 33(13) Deregulation Act 2015

"relevant notice" means—

(a) a notice served under section 11 of the Housing Act 2004 (improvement notices relating to category 1 hazards),

(b) a notice served under section 12 of that Act (improvement notices relating to category 2 hazards), or

(c) a notice served under section 40(7) of that Act (emergency remedial action)

2. **Was the landlord served with an improvement notice or a notice for emergency remedial action prior to the hearing?**

   (i) Was the landlord served with a notice under Section 11, 12, or 40(7) Housing Act 2004 prior to the hearing, and was this as a result of a complaint by the tenant to the Local Authority about the housing conditions, and had the tenant made substantially the same complaint to the landlord in writing prior to the service of the Section 21 notice?

   (ii) If so, then DEFENCE:

   - In these circumstances, the Section 21 notice served is invalid (s33(2) Deregulation Act 2015).

(iii) DISCRETION OF THE COURT:

   - None. No discretion to dispense with service of a Section 21 notice.

   - The court "must strike out" the claim in these circumstances (s33(6) Deregulation Act 2015).

Section 33(2) Deregulation Act 2015

A section 21 notice given in relation to an assured shorthold tenancy of a dwelling-house in England is invalid where—

(a) before the section 21 notice was given, the tenant made a complaint in writing to the landlord regarding the condition of the dwelling-house at the time of the complaint,

(b) the landlord—

...

(iii) gave a section 21 notice in relation to the dwelling-house following the complaint,

(c) the tenant then made a complaint to the relevant local housing authority about the same, or substantially the same, subject matter as the complaint to the landlord,

(d) the relevant local housing authority served a relevant notice in relation to the dwelling-house in response to the complaint, and

(e) if the section 21 notice was not given before the tenant's complaint to the local housing authority, it was given before the service of the relevant notice.

[see above for authority that the relevant notices are notices under ss11, 12, or 40(7) Housing Act 2004].

Section 33(6) Deregulation Act 2015

The court must strike out proceedings for an order for possession under section 21 of the Housing Act 1988 in relation to a dwelling-house in England if, before the order is made, the section 21 notice that would otherwise require the court to make an order for possession in relation to the dwelling-house has become invalid under subsection (2).

LICENSING REQUIREMENTS (SELECTIVE LICENSING FOR RENTAL)

1. **Does the property require licensing under Section 85 Housing Act 2004?**

YES if:

- It is in an area designated by the Local Authority under Section 80 Housing Act 2004 as requiring selective licensing (check the Local Authority's website for designated areas / streets) (s79 Housing Act 2004);
- It is (or self-contained dwellings within it are individually) let under a single tenancy or licence (s79(2)(b) Housing Act 2004).

NOT APPLICABLE to:

- Social housing (s79(3) Housing Act 2004);
- HMOs to which HMO licensing applies (s85(1)(a) Housing Act 2004);
- Properties to which there is a temporary exemption notice in force under Section 86 Housing Act 2004 (s85(1)(b) Housing Act 2004).

(i) If the property requires licensing under Section 85 Housing Act 2004, was it so licensed (or did one of the following circumstances apply) at the date of service of the Section 21 notice?

- A temporary exemption was in place under Section 86 Housing Act 2004 (s98(2), s96(1)(b) and s96(2)(a) Housing Act 2004);
- An application for a licence had been made and had either not yet been decided by the Local Authority, or the time limit for an appeal of a negative decision had not yet

expired, or a negative decision had been appealed and the appeal had not yet been decided (s98(2), s96(1)(b), s96(2)(b), s95(7) and s95(8) Housing Act 2004).

(ii) If not, then DEFENCE:

- This property requires selective licensing and is an unlicensed property (/ was an unlicensed property at the date of service of the purported Section 21 notice);
- "No Section 21 notice may be given" at a time that a property requiring licensing is unlicensed (s98(1) Housing Act 2004);
- The Section 21 notice is therefore invalid.

(iii) DISCRETION OF THE COURT:

- None – "No section 21 notice may be given" (mandatory wording). Cannot dispense with service of a s21 notice.

<u>Section 79 Housing Act 2004</u>

(1) This Part provides for houses to be licensed by local housing authorities where—

(a) they are houses to which this Part applies (see subsection (2)), and

(b) they are required to be licensed under this Part (see section 85(1)).

(2) This Part applies to a house if—

(a) it is in an area that is for the time being designated under section 80 as subject to selective licensing, and

(b) the whole of it is occupied either—

(i) under a single tenancy or licence that is not an exempt tenancy or licence under subsection (3) or (4), or

(ii) under two or more tenancies or licences in respect of different dwellings contained in it, none of which is an exempt tenancy or licence under subsection (3) or (4).

(3) A tenancy or licence is an exempt tenancy or licence if—

(a) it is granted by a non-profit registered provider of social housing,

(b) it is granted by a profit-making registered provider of social housing in respect of social housing (within the meaning of Part 2 of the Housing and Regeneration Act 2008), or

(c) it is granted by a body which is registered as a social landlord under Part 1 of the Housing Act 1996....

Section 80 Housing Act 2004

(1) A local housing authority may designate either—

(a) the area of their district, or

(b) an area in their district, as subject to selective licensing, if the requirements of subsections (2) and (9) are met.

...

Section 85 Housing Act 2004

(1) Every Part 3 house must be licensed under this Part unless—

(a) it is an HMO to which Part 2 applies (see section 55(2)), or

(b) a temporary exemption notice is in force in relation to it under section 86, or

(c) a management order is in force in relation to it under Chapter 1 or 2 of Part 4.

Section 95 Housing Act 2004

...

(7)... [an] application is "effective" at a particular time if at that time it has not been withdrawn, and either—

(a) the authority have not decided whether to... grant a licence, in pursuance of the... application, or

(b) if they have decided not to do so, one of the conditions set out in subsection (8) is met.

(8) The conditions are—

(a) that the period for appealing against the decision of the authority not to... grant such a... licence (or against any relevant decision of the appropriate tribunal) has not expired, or

(b) that an appeal has been brought against the authority's decision (or against any relevant decision of such a tribunal) and the appeal has not been determined or withdrawn.

Section 96 Housing Act 2004

(1) For the purposes of this section a house is an "unlicensed house" if—

(a) it is required to be licensed under this Part but is not so licensed, and

(b) neither of the conditions in subsection (2) is satisfied.

(2) The conditions are—

(a) that a notification has been duly given in respect of the house under section... 86(1) and that notification is still effective (as defined by section 95(7));

(b) that an application for a licence has been duly made in respect of the house under section 87 and that application is still effective (as so defined).

...

Section 98 Housing Act 2004

(1) No section 21 notice may be given in relation to a shorthold tenancy of the whole or part of an unlicensed house so long as it remains such a house.

(2) In this section—

...

"unlicensed house" has the same meaning as in section 96 of this Act.

LICENSING REQUIREMENTS (HOUSES IN MULTIPLE OCCUPANCY)

1. Does the property require licensing under Section 61 Housing Act 2004?

YES if:

- The property consists of 3 or more storeys and is rented to 5 or more people living in 2 or more households (s55(2)(a) Housing Act 2004 and Art. 3 of the Licensing of Houses in Multiple Occupation (Prescribed Descriptions) (England) Order 2006)) (= MANDATORY LICENSING);

  Or

- The property is an HMO within the definition of ss254-260 Housing Act 2004 as subject to the exclusions in Schedule 14 Housing Act 2004 (the most common circumstance being where the property is shared by 3 or more people living in 2 or more households and sharing basic living facilities) AND the property is in a designated area subject to ADDITIONAL LICENSING by the Local Authority (check the council's website) (s55(2)(b) Housing Act 2004).

NOT APPLICABLE to:

- The exclusions in Schedule 14 Housing Act 2004 (e.g. social housing, student halls) (see the statute).

- There is a temporary exemption notice in force in relation to the property under Section 62 Housing Act 2004 (s61(1)(a) Housing Act 2004).

(i) If the property requires licensing under Section 61 Housing Act 2004, was it so licensed (or did one of the following circumstances apply) at the date of service of the Section 21 notice?

- A temporary exemption was in place under Section 62 Housing Act 2004 (s75(2), s73(1)(b) and s73(2)(a) Housing Act 2004);

- An application for a licence had been made and had either not yet been decided by the Local Authority, or the time limit for an appeal of a negative decision had not yet expired, or a negative decision had been appealed and the appeal had not yet been decided (s75(2), s73(1)(b), s73(2)(b), s72(8) and s72(9) Housing Act 2004)

(ii) If not, then DEFENCE:

- This property requires HMO mandatory / additional licensing and is an unlicensed property (/ was an unlicensed property at the date of service of the purported Section 21 notice);

- "No Section 21 notice may be given" at a time that a property requiring licensing is unlicensed (s75(1) Housing Act 2004);

- The Section 21 notice is therefore invalid.

(iii) DISCRETION OF THE COURT:

- None – "No section 21 notice may be given" (mandatory wording). Cannot dispense with service of a s21 notice.

<u>**Section 55 Housing Act 2004**</u>

…

(2) This Part applies to the following HMOs in the case of each local housing authority—

(a) any HMO in the authority's district which falls within any prescribed description of HMO, and

(b) if an area is for the time being designated by the authority under section 56 as subject to additional licensing, any HMO in that area which falls within any description of HMO specified in the designation.

...

Section 61 Housing Act 2004

(1) Every HMO to which this Part applies must be licensed under this Part unless—

(a) a temporary exemption notice is in force in relation to it under section 62, or

(b) an interim or final management order is in force in relation to it under Chapter 1 of Part 4.

Section 72 Housing Act 2004

...

(8) ... [an] application is "effective" at a particular time if at that time it has not been withdrawn, and either—

(a) the authority have not decided whether to... grant a licence, in pursuance of the... application, or

(b) if they have decided not to do so, one of the conditions set out in subsection (9) is met.

(9) The conditions are—

(a) that the period for appealing against the decision of the authority not to... grant such a... licence (or against any relevant decision of the appropriate tribunal) has not expired, or

(b) that an appeal has been brought against the authority's decision (or against any relevant decision of such a tribunal) and the appeal has not been determined or withdrawn.

…

Section 75 Housing Act 2004

(1) No section 21 notice may be given in relation to a shorthold tenancy of a part of an unlicensed HMO so long as it remains such an HMO.

(2) In this section—

…

"unlicensed HMO" has the same meaning as in section 73 of this Act.

Section 73 Housing Act 2004

(1) For the purposes of this section an HMO is an "unlicensed HMO" if—

(a) it is required to be licensed under this Part but is not so licensed, and

(b) neither of the conditions in subsection (2) is satisfied.

(2) The conditions are—

(a) that a notification has been duly given in respect of the HMO under section 62(1) and that notification is still effective (as defined by section 72(8));

(b) that an application for a licence has been duly made in respect of the HMO under section 63 and that application is still effective (as so defined).

…

Art. 3 of the Licensing of Houses in Multiple Occupation (Prescribed Descriptions) (England) Order 2006))

(1) An HMO is of a prescribed description for the purpose of section 55(2)(a) of the Act where it satisfies the conditions described in paragraph (2).

(2) The conditions referred to in paragraph (1) are that—

(a) the HMO or any part of it comprises three storeys or more;

(b) it is occupied by five or more persons; and

(c) it is occupied by persons living in two or more single households.

...

PROHIBITED FEES

1. Has the tenant or guarantor paid a prohibited fee?

(i) Has the tenant or any guarantor (etc.) paid ANY fee in respect of the tenancy which is not a permitted fee?

Permitted Fees	Limits	Authority
Rent	The usual rent going forward – i.e. if the usual rent is X, but the first rent is X+Y, then Y is a prohibited payment.	Para. 1(1) Sch. 1 Tenant Fees Act 2019
Deposit	5 weeks' rent where the annual rent is less than £50,000 6 weeks' rent where the annual rent is £50,000 or more	Para. 2(1) Sch. 1 Tenant Fees Act 2019
Holding Deposit	1 week's rent Also, if this is a second holding deposit paid in respect of the same property – the earlier one not having been repaid (without lawful excuse – see paras 6 -12 Sch. 2).	Para. 3(1) Sch. 1 Tenant Fees Act 2019
A fee for replacing a lost key OR a fee for late payment of rent	Replacing a lost key – costs reasonably incurred If rent is 14 days late, then a fee for late payment of rent amounting to max. of base rate plus 3%, accruing daily from the day after the rent fell due	Para. 4(1) Sch. 1 Tenant Fees Act 2019

Damages for breach of agreement	N/A	Para. 5 Sch. 1 Tenant Fees Act 2019
A payment relating to a tenant's request for a variation, or assignment	£50, or reasonable costs	Para. 6(1) Sch. 1 Tenant Fees Act 2019
A payment to a LL relating to a tenant's request for a surrender	The LL's losses	Para. 7(1) Sch. 1 Tenant Fees Act 2019
A payment to a letting agency relating to a tenant's request for a surrender	The letting agency's reasonable costs	Para. 7(3) Sch. 1 Tenant Fees Act 2019
A payment in respect of council tax, utilities, telephone or internet, television licence	Where payment is made to the LL, reasonable costs	Paras. 8(1), 9(1), 10(1), 11(1) Sch. 1 Tenant Fees Act 2019

(ii) If yes, then DEFENCE:

- Any payment which is not specifically a permitted payment is a prohibited payment (s3 Tenant Fees Act 2019).

- Landlords must not require a prohibited payment (s1(1) Tenant Fees Act 2019).

- The Tenant Fees Act applies to all tenancies to all payments made on or after 1 June 2020, or for payments made on or after 1 June 2019 for tenancies that commenced or were renewed on or after that date (Reg. 3(a) The Tenant Fees Act 2019 (Commencement No. 3) Regulations 2019, and s30(3) Tenant Fees Act 2019).

- "No Section 21 notice may be given" until the prohibited payment has been returned to the tenant (or relevant person) (s17(3) Tenant Fees Act 2019) UNLESS all or the other part of the prohibited payment has with the consent of the tenant (or relevant person) been applied towards the rent or the deposit (s17(4) and (5) Tenant Fees Act 2019).

- The Section 21 notice is therefore invalid and the claim must be dismissed.

(iii) DISCRETION OF THE COURT:

- None. Mandatory wording ("no Section 21 notice may be given") (s17(3) Tenant Fees Act 2019).

- Cannot dispense with service of a Section 21 notice.

<u>Section 1 Tenant Fees Act 2019</u>

(1) A landlord must not require a relevant person to make a prohibited payment to the landlord in connection with a tenancy of housing in England.

<u>Section 17 Tenant Fees Act 2019</u>

(3) No section 21 notice may be given in relation to the tenancy so long as all or part of the prohibited payment or holding deposit has not been repaid to the relevant person.

<u>Section 30 Tenant Fees Act 2019</u>

(3) Subsection… (6)… appl[ies] in relation to a provision of a tenancy agreement entered into before the coming into force of section 1 if, had the agreement been entered into after that time, that section would have applied in relation to the provision or a requirement imposed pursuant to it.

…

(6) If, after the end of the period of one year beginning with the date on which section 1 comes into force—

(a) the landlord or a letting agent accepts a payment from a relevant person pursuant to the provision…

the landlord or letting agent is to be treated for the purposes of this Act as having required the relevant person to make a prohibited payment of that amount at that time.

Regulation 3 The Tenant Fees Act 2019 (Commencement No. 3) Regulations 2019

The following provisions of the Act come into force on 1st June 2019 —

(a) section 1 (prohibitions applying to landlords)

…

CHAPTER FOURTEEN

SECTION 8 (THE RENT ARREARS GROUNDS) SPECIFIC DEFENCES

MAKING OUT GROUNDS 8, 10, AND 11

1. **Is the Ground relied upon made out?**

   (i) Is the ground relied upon made out?

<table>
<tr><th>GROUND:</th><th>8</th><th>10</th><th>11</th></tr>
<tr><td rowspan="3">LEGAL TEST:</td><td>1. At least 2 months' rent* is lawfully due at the date of the service of the NOSP</td><td>1. Some rent is lawfully due at the date of the service of the NOSP (except where service of the NOSP has been dispensed with)</td><td>1. There has been persistent delay in the payment of rent lawfully due</td></tr>
<tr><td rowspan="2">2. At least 2 months' rent* is lawfully due at the date of the hearing</td><td>2. Some rent is lawfully due at the date proceedings are commenced</td><td rowspan="2">2. It would be reasonable to make a possession order</td></tr>
<tr><td>3. It would be reasonable to make a possession order</td></tr>
</table>

* The test is: (1) if rent is paid monthly then 2 months' rent is lawfully due, (2) if weekly then 8 weeks' rent is lawfully due, (3) if quarterly then

1 quarter's rent is lawfully due and is more than 3 months late, (4) if yearly then 3 months' rent is lawfully due and is more than 3 months late.

N.B. Whether or not rent is "lawfully due" is the subject of all of the other defences in this chapter.

AUTHORITY: Grounds 8, 10, and 11 of Schedule 2 of the Housing Act 1988, and (as to the reasonableness test) s7(4) Housing Act 1988.

(ii) If not, then DEFENCE:

- "The court shall not make an order for possession of a dwelling-house let on an assured tenancy except on one or more of the grounds set out in Schedule 2 to this Act" (s7(1) Housing Act 1988).
- The ground in question is not made out and the court therefore has no power to make an order.
- The claimant has no basis for possession and the claim must be dismissed.

(iii) DISCRETION OF THE COURT:

- If the ground is not made out, then no discretion (mandatory wording of s7(1) Housing Act 1988 – "the court shall not make").
- If ground 8 is made out, then no discretion (mandatory wording of s7(3) Housing Act 1988 – "the court shall make").
- If grounds 10 or 11 are made out, the court has full discretion ("the court may make" – s7(4) Housing Act 1988).
- If ground 10 (only) is (only) not made out because there were no arrears lawfully due at the date of service of the

NOSP, the court may circumnavigate this problem by dispensing with service of the Section 8 notice.

Section 7 Housing Act 1988

(1) The court shall not make an order for possession of a dwelling-house let on an assured tenancy except on one or more of the grounds set out in Schedule 2 to this Act...

...

(3) If the court is satisfied that any of the grounds in Part I of Schedule 2 to this Act is established then... the court shall make an order for possession.

(4) If the court is satisfied that any of the grounds in Part II of Schedule 2 to this Act is established, then... the court may make an order for possession if it considers it reasonable to do so.

Part I, Schedule 2 Housing Act 1988

...

GROUND 8 Both at the date of the service of the notice under section 8 of this Act relating to the proceedings for possession and at the date of the hearing—

(a) if rent is payable weekly or fortnightly, at least eight weeks' rent is unpaid;

(b) if rent is payable monthly, at least two months' rent is unpaid;

(c) if rent is payable quarterly, at least one quarter's rent is more than three months in arrears; and

(d) if rent is payable yearly, at least three months' rent is more than three months in arrears;

and for the purpose of this ground "rent" means rent lawfully due from the tenant.

Part II, Schedule 2 Housing Act 1988

...

GROUND 10 Some rent lawfully due from the tenant—

(a) is unpaid on the date on which the proceedings for possession are begun; and

(b) except where subsection (1)(b) of section 8 of this Act applies, was in arrears at the date of the service of the notice under that section relating to those proceedings.

...

GROUND 11 Whether or not any rent is in arrears on the date on which proceedings for possession are begun, the tenant has persistently delayed paying rent which has become lawfully due.

SECTION 48 NOTICE

1. **Has the Landlord furnished the tenant with an address in England or Wales for service (a Section 48 Notice)?**

(i) Has the landlord furnished the tenant with an address in England or Wales for service (a "Section 48 Notice") prior to or at the same time as service of the Section 8 notice?

- NOTE – there is no prescribed form for a Section 48 notice. It only needs to be in writing and does not need to specify any reference to "section 48" (Rogan v Woodfield Building Services, Court of Appeal (1994)). Once furnished, all rent up until that point immediately becomes lawfully due.

(ii) If not, then DEFENCE:

- To furnish such notice is a requirement pursuant to s48(1) Landlord and Tenant Act 1987).

- Until such notice is provided, no rent is lawfully due and therefore the legal tests for grounds 8, 10 or 11 cannot be met (s48(2) Landlord and Tenant Act 1987).

- Unless the s48 notice was served before or at the same time as the Section 8 notice, Grounds 8 and 10 can never be relied upon in these proceedings as no rent was lawfully due at the date of service of the Section 8 notice (Marath & Anor v Macgillivray, Court of Appeal (1996)).

(iii) DISCRETION OF THE COURT:

- While the problem persists, none. A mandatory requirement. If no rent is lawfully due then none of the grounds for possession 8, 10 or 11 can be satisfied.

- If the s48 notice was not served at the same time or prior to the service of the Section 8 notice, then Ground 8 will necessarily be excluded and this cannot be cured by subsequent service of the s48 notice. If the s48 notice is subsequently served (still prior to the hearing), then (although the Section 8 notice itself still may not be relied upon) for the purposes of Grounds 10 and 11 service of the Section 8 notice can be dispensed with if the court considers it just and equitable to do so (s8(1)(b) Housing Act 1988).

Section 48 Landlord and Tenant Act 1987

(1) A landlord of premises to which this Part applies shall by notice furnish the tenant with an address in England and Wales at which notices (including notices in proceedings) may be served on him by the tenant.

(2) Where a landlord of any such premises fails to comply with subsection (1), any rent… otherwise due from the tenant to the landlord shall… be treated for all purposes as not being due from the tenant to the landlord at any time before the landlord does comply with that subsection.

Rogan v Woodfield Building Services, Court of Appeal (1994)

LORD JUSTICE SMITH: What the section requires is that the tenant is told, so that he knows, the landlord's name and address in England or Wales at which he can be served with notices. If the name and address is stated in the lease or tenancy agreement without limitation or qualification, it is a necessary implication that he can be communicated with at that address and hence it is a place to which notices can be sent. The section does not require that the notice shall state that it is the address at which notices can be served. The mischief at which the section was aimed was the problem created when the landlord's identity was not known and / or the tenant did not know of an address within the jurisdiction to which notices could be sent and proceedings served".

Marath & Anor v Macgillivray, Court of Appeal (1996)

SIR IAIN GLIDEWELL: "… [R]ent is not due until a notice containing the landlord's address for service of notices upon him has been served in accordance with s48 of the Landlord and Tenant Act 1987. It follows that it is a requirement that such a notice must have been served before the s8 notice was served".

DEFENCE OF SET-OFF BY WAY OF A COUNTERCLAIM: DISREPAIR / HOUSING CONDITIONS

NOTA BENE – Although I have included it below for completeness, on the court duty desk you are unlikely to have time to consider what breach has occurred exactly (i.e. a breach of s11, s9A, an express repairing term in the tenancy, or a common law implied term). You will need more evidence than you have on court duty desk anyway. In this case, you may prefer (or be compelled) to skip straight to the section titled "BEGIN HERE IF YOU ARE SHORT OF TIME below in order to value the potential counterclaim. For the same reason, I have not included extracts / quotations from the cited authorities in this first section – these are the "flesh on the bone" and can be studied in more detail when you are back in the office.

1. **Is there disrepair or poor housing conditions at the property which may give rise to a counterclaim?**

   (i) Is there disrepair or poor housing conditions at the property which amounts to a breach of:

   - **Section 11 Landlord and Tenant Act 1985 (repairing obligations)**

The obligation of the LL to keep in repair:

S11 Requirement to keep in repair...	Including
The structure and exterior of the dwelling-house (including drains, gutters and external pipes)	Walls, floors, window frames and windowpanes (Ball v Plumber, Court of Appeal (1879)), drains, pipes
The installations in the dwelling-house for the supply of water, gas and electricity and for sanitation (including basins, sinks, baths and sanitary conveniences)	Water pipes, gas pipes, electrics, basins, sinks, baths, toilets
The installations in the dwelling-house for space heating and heating water	Fixed heaters and water heaters

Does NOT include problems with condensation (caused by warm internal air hitting the cold external walls / windows of the building) and therefore NOT mould caused by said condensation (Quick v Taff Ely Borough Council, Court of Appeal (1986)).

Mould is only a potential symptom of disrepair and is not disrepair in itself – it can only be dealt with under this head if it is identifiably caused by disrepair to any of the items above.

"Repair" does NOT include "betterment", only maintenance.

- **Section 9A Landlord and Tenant Act 1985 (fitness for human habitation)**

The obligation (since 20 March 2020 for all tenancies, or from the commencement date for any tenancies granted on or after 20 March 2019) that the premises must be fit for human habitation at the beginning of the term of the lease and that it must remain fit for human habitation throughout the term of the lease, such that it is NOT defective so as to be not reasonably suitable for occupation in that condition having regard to:

Repair
Stability
Freedom from damp
Internal arrangement
Natural lighting
Ventilation
Water supply
Drainage and sanitary conveniences
Facilities for preparation and cooking of food and for the disposal of waste water

<table>
<tr><td rowspan="10">A prescribed hazard</td><td>Hazards prescribed by the Housing Health and Safety Rating System (England) Regulations 2005 made pursuant to Section 2 of the Housing Act 2004:
A hazard is a risk of harm (as defined and categorised in the Regulations) arising from:</td></tr>
<tr><td>Damp and mould growth
1. Exposure to house dust mites, damp, mould or fungal growths.</td></tr>
<tr><td>Excess cold
2. Exposure to low temperatures.</td></tr>
<tr><td>Excess heat
3. Exposure to high temperatures.</td></tr>
<tr><td>Asbestos and MMF
4. Exposure to asbestos fibres or manufactured mineral fibres.</td></tr>
<tr><td>Biocides
5. Exposure to chemicals used to treat timber and mould growth.</td></tr>
<tr><td>Carbon monoxide and fuel combustion products
6. Exposure to—
(a) carbon monoxide;
(b) nitrogen dioxide;
(c) sulphur dioxide and smoke.</td></tr>
<tr><td>Lead
7. The ingestion of lead.</td></tr>
<tr><td>Radiation
8. Exposure to radiation.</td></tr>
<tr><td>Uncombusted fuel gas
9. Exposure to uncombusted fuel gas.</td></tr>
</table>

	Volatile organic compounds 10. Exposure to volatile organic compounds.
	Crowding and space 11. A lack of adequate space for living and sleeping.
	Entry by intruders 12. Difficulties in keeping the dwelling or HMO secure against unauthorised entry.
	Lighting 13. A lack of adequate lighting.
	Noise 14. Exposure to noise.
	Domestic hygiene, pests and refuse 15.(1) Poor design, layout or construction such that the dwelling or HMO cannot readily be kept clean. (2) Exposure to pests. (3) An inadequate provision for the hygienic storage and disposal of household waste.
	Food safety 16. An inadequate provision of facilities for the storage, preparation and cooking of food.
	Personal hygiene, sanitation and drainage 17. An inadequate provision of— (a) facilities for maintaining good personal hygiene; (b) sanitation and drainage.
	Water supply 18. An inadequate supply of water free from contamination, for drinking and other domestic purposes.
	Falls associated with baths etc 19. Falls associated with toilets, baths, showers or other washing facilities.

	Falling on level surfaces etc 20. Falling on any level surface or falling between surfaces where the change in level is less than 300 millimetres.
	Falling on stairs etc 21. Falling on stairs, steps or ramps where the change in level is 300 millimetres or more.
	Falling between levels 22. Falling between levels where the difference in levels is 300 millimetres or more.
	Electrical hazards 23. Exposure to electricity.
	Fire 24. Exposure to uncontrolled fire and associated smoke.
	Flames, hot surfaces etc 25. Contact with— (a) controlled fire or flames; (b) hot objects, liquid or vapours.
	Collision and entrapment 26. Collision with, or entrapment of body parts in, doors, windows or other architectural features.
	Explosions 27. An explosion at the dwelling or HMO.
	Position and operability of amenities etc 28. The position, location and operability of amenities, fittings and equipment.
	Structural collapse and falling elements 29. The collapse of the whole or part of the dwelling or HMO.

AUTHORITY: s10(1) Landlord and Tenant Act 1985 and, for the prescribed hazards, Schedule I of the Housing Health and Safety Rating System (England) Regulations 2005.

You will note that mould which cannot be linked to s11 disrepair may nonetheless found a claim for unfitness for human habitation, as might condensation (under the "ventilation" head).

NOTE that for the category of "prescribed hazards", the hazard is only prescribed if there is a risk of "harm". Levels of harm are categorised in the regulations in non-exhaustive lists by type. There is no requirement for a risk of "harm" for any of the other categories.

Categories of harm:

Class I	1. A Class I harm is such extreme harm as is reasonably foreseeable as a result of the hazard in question, including— (a) death from any cause; (b) lung cancer; (c) mesothelioma and other malignant tumours; (d) permanent paralysis below the neck; (e) regular severe pneumonia; (f) permanent loss of consciousness; (g) 80% burn injuries.
Class II	2. A Class II harm is such severe harm as is reasonably foreseeable as a result of the hazard in question, including— (a) cardio-respiratory disease; (b) asthma; (c) non-malignant respiratory diseases; (d) lead poisoning; (e) anaphylactic shock; (f) cryptosporidiosis; (g) legionnaires disease;

	(h) myocardial infarction; (i) mild stroke; (j) chronic confusion; (k) regular severe fever; (l) loss of a hand or foot; (m) serious fractures; (n) serious burns; (o) loss of consciousness for days.
Class III	3. A Class III harm is such serious harm as is reasonably foreseeable as a result of the hazard in question, including— (a) eye disorders; (b) rhinitis; (c) hypertension; (d) sleep disturbance; (e) neuropsychological impairment; (f) sick building syndrome; (g) regular and persistent dermatitis, including contact dermatitis; (h) allergy; (i) gastro-enteritis; (j) diarrhoea; (k) vomiting; (l) chronic severe stress; (m) mild heart attack; (n) malignant but treatable skin cancer; (o) loss of a finger; (p) fractured skull and severe concussion; (q) serious puncture wounds to head or body; (r) severe burns to hands; (s) serious strain or sprain injuries; (t) regular and severe migraine.

Class IV	4. A Class IV harm is such moderate harm as is reasonably foreseeable as a result of the hazard in question, including— (a) pleural plaques; (b) occasional severe discomfort; (c) benign tumours; (d) occasional mild pneumonia; (e) broken finger; (f) slight concussion; (g) moderate cuts to face or body; (h) severe bruising to body; (i) regular serious coughs or colds.

AUTHORITY: Schedule II of the Housing Health and Safety Rating System (England) Regulations 2005.

You will note that damp may amount to unfitness under its own category, "freedom from damp", or as a prescribed hazard of "damp and mould growth" – but the latter only if harm of one of the levels of categorisation is caused. That, is, as a minimum, the damp and mould growth must have caused "regular serious coughs or colds" or "occasional severe discomfort" or "occasional mild pneumonia" (etc.) to amount to a prescribed hazard.

For ALL of the above categories speaking to fitness (first table), including prescribed hazards, the housing conditions only amount to unfitness for human habitation "**if, and only if, it is so far defective in one or more of those matters that it is not reasonably suitable for occupation in that condition**" (s10(1) Landlord and Tenant Act 1985).

- **An express repairing term of the tenancy agreement**

INCLUDING:

A COVENANT FOR THE LL TO:	INCLUDES / COVERS:	AUTHORITY:
"maintain the dwelling in good condition"	condensation and mould growth even where that is not attributable to disrepair	Welsh v Greenwich LBC, Court of Appeal (2001)
"take reasonable steps to keep the estate and common parts clean and tidy"	Inadequate rubbish disposal facilities even where there is no disrepair	Long v Southwark LBC, Court of Appeal (2002)

- **A repairing term implied by the common law**

INCLUDING:

A COVENANT FOR THE LL TO:	INCLUDES / COVERS:	AUTHORITY:
Maintain any part of a property still in the LL's control (i.e. not demised) to prevent injury or damage to the tenant and the demised premises	Damp in a part of the property still in the LL's control	Cockburn v Smith, Court of Appeal (1924).
Maintain any common parts which the tenant has a contractual right to use	A shared bathroom or toilet	Miller v Emcer Products Ltd, Court of Appeal (1955).
Maintain facilities necessary for use by the tenant	Lifts, rubbish chutes	Liverpool City Council v Irwin, House of Lords (1976).

- **The implied (may also be express) covenant for quiet enjoyment**

Where no express term may be relied upon, this is a term implied by the common law (Jenkins v Jackson, High Court (Chancery Division) (1888)). This may be breached by disrepair or a failure by the landlord to prevent disturbance caused by works, for example:

EXAMPLE	AUTHORITY
LL's failure to keep the property watertight, causing damage to the tenant's flat.	Booth v Thomas, Court of Appeal (1926).
Any part of the property still in the LL's control causing interference with the demised premises.	Chevron Petroleum (UK) Ltd v Post Office, Court of Session (1987) [Scottish authority].
A failure to take reasonable steps to prevent disturbance during works.	N/A

(ii) Is the landlord on actual or implied notice of the disrepair / housing conditions / breach of express term?

ACTUAL NOTICE	1. LL was actually informed (preferably in writing). [LL does not have to be told exactly the extent of the disrepair There is no need for notice to specify the extent of the disrepair (Griffin v Pillet, High Court (King's Bench Division) (1925)].
IMPLIED NOTICE	1. LL has inspected the property and s11 disrepair should have been obvious (even though not pointed out) (Kerr as trustee of the Haie Estate and Anor v Maass, High Court (Chancery Division) (2019)). 2. LL's agent is on actual notice; LL (principal) is on implied notice. 3. The disrepair is in common parts not part of the demise (i.e. still within the control of the LL). (British Telecommunications plc v Sun Life plc, Court of Appeal (1996).

(iii) Is there therefore a counterclaim available that may amount to an arguable defence as per Birmingham City Council v Stephenson (Court of Appeal, 2016) or a defence on grounds which appear to be substantial as per CPR r. 55.8(2) (see introductory chapter)?

NOTE 1 – Damages for the above breaches are all contractual. They are to put the tenant in the position he would have been in had the landlord not breached his contractual repairing obligations. The "value" amounts to the distress, discomfort and inconvenience suffered by the tenant as a result of the disrepair (Wallace v Manchester City Council, Court of Appeal (1998)), and is equivalent to the loss of amenity value (Moorjani v Durban Estates Ltd, Court of Appeal (2015)).

NOTE 2 – in the cut and thrust of court duty advice use the same calculation for all heads of damage above, HOWEVER, note that for unfitness for human habitation, it is arguable that if a property is indeed "unfit for human habitation" then the loss of amenity is total, requiring a 100% rent rebate. There is no higher court case law on this.

BEGIN HERE IF YOU ARE SHORT OF TIME:

If you are satisfied (instructed, ideally with evidence) that there are conditions which may amount to a breach of the landlord's repairing obligations or a breach of related obligations, and you do not have time to specifically identify what the breach may be, then start at this point. Once you have completed the following section it will be helpful if you refer to the above so that you can articulate / approximate what the breach is likely to be.

1. What is the relevant rent at the property?

- Social tenancy: full social rent (including that portion paid by HB / UC)
- Private tenancy: private rent

£........... per month / week

2. When was the LL notified of the disrepair? By when should the LL have corrected the disrepair? How long therefore has the disrepair been actionable?

.... months / weeks

3. What is the value of the relevant rent for that entire period?

£..

4. How many rooms constitute the property? What percentage of the property does each room represent?

[Apportion equal shares to each bedroom, living room, dining room. The other rooms (kitchen, bathroom) should together account for one equal share].

<table>
<tr><td>Bedroom 1</td><td>25%</td></tr>
<tr><td>Bedroom 2</td><td>25%</td></tr>
<tr><td>Living Room</td><td>25%</td></tr>
<tr><td>Kitchen</td><td rowspan="2">25%</td></tr>
<tr><td>Bathroom</td></tr>
</table>

<table>
<tr><td>Bedroom 1</td><td>33%</td></tr>
<tr><td>Living Room</td><td>33%</td></tr>
<tr><td>Kitchen</td><td rowspan="2">33%</td></tr>
<tr><td>Bathroom</td></tr>
</table>

<table>
<tr><td>Bedroom 1</td><td>50%</td></tr>
<tr><td>Kitchen</td><td rowspan="2">50%</td></tr>
<tr><td>Bathroom</td></tr>
</table>

5. How badly affected (in terms of the tenant's usage) is each room affected by the housing conditions?

- Completely unusable = 100%
- Somewhere in between = [use your discretion. 50% may be a sensible place to start – but keep the maths simple].
- Completely unaffected = 0%

6. Given the percentage effect on each room, and the percentage of the whole property which each room represents, what is the percentage effect on the property as a whole?

.... percent (%)

7. Considering the fact that the claim is effectively for loss of amenity, are there any exacerbating factors that apply? If so, increase the percentage effect as appropriate, to give:

.... percent (%)

[For example:

- The tenant has children living with him (especially young children), and particularly if:
    - It is embarrassing to have friends / family "come round" because of the disrepair;
    - The disrepair makes it difficult to do homework;
    - The disrepair makes it difficult to wash (e.g. if there is no hot water);
    - The disrepair is such that the parents are scared for the safety of their children;
- The tenant has children who should be living with him but who cannot due to the disrepair (meaning that custody remains with the other parent, or with social services etc.);
- The tenant or family spends a lot of time at home – for example, is housebound, or works from home].

8. Applying this percentage to the value of the full rent for the actionable period, what is the potential value of the claim?

£...

9. Are there any other contractual or tortious claims available? Add the value of these to the value of this claim to give the following subtotal.

£...

10. Increase the total by the Simmons v Castle 10% uplift.

£...

11. Are there any special damages that could be claimed? What is the value?

£...

12. What is (what may be) the total value of the claim?

£...

13. What are the arrears claimed at the date of the hearing?

£...

14. What are the arrears claimed at the date of service of the Section 8 notice?

£...

15. What are the arrears claimed at the date the proceedings were begun?

£..

16. Does a Defence arise?

...

17. If so, then DEFENCE:

- The existence of a counterclaim impugns the legal title to the arrears, providing a direct defence of set off.
- Up to the value of the set off (once determined), therefore, the arrears claimed are not lawfully due, and cannot be relied upon to found a possession order on grounds 8, 10 or 11.
- EXCLUDING GROUND 8: In order to exclude Ground 8, the counterclaim would only have to have a value of X, since that would bring the arrears claimed at the date of service of the NOSP down to below 2 months.
- EXCLUDING GROUND 10: In order to exclude Ground 10, the counterclaim would only have to have a value of Y, since this would extinguish the arrears claimed at the date of service of the NOSP (service of which has not been dispensed with) or where service of the notice has been dispensed with, would have to have a value of Z, since this would extinguish the arrears claimed at the date proceedings were commenced. In any event it would not be reasonable to make a possession order at a time when the claimant himself is in breach of his own contractual obligations.
- EXCLUDING GROUND 11: Any value of a counterclaim would necessarily impugn the claimant's

ability to rely on Ground 11 since whether a particular portion of arrears were lawfully due, and whether this amounts to persistent lateness of paying rent that is lawfully due, would require careful consideration and cross referencing of timelines as they relate to: 1. rent falling due, 2. the LL being on notice of disrepair and liability arising, and 3. rent being paid. In any event it would not be reasonable to make a possession order at a time when the claimant himself is in breach of his own contractual obligations.

- It is not a fanciful suggestion that the counterclaim may be worth at least X% of the rent for the actionable period, which would amount to a value of X [and together with any other heads of counterclaim would come to Y]. This would benefit from the Simmons v Castle 10% uplift and interest, [and any special damages] all of which add up to impugn the legal title to the arrears claimed to the value of Z. It is not fanciful to suggest that each of Grounds 8, 10 and 11 would be excluded.

- The evidence / testimony before the court today suggests therefore a Defence on grounds that appear to be substantial or at least a Defence which is arguable and not fanciful, and therefore an opportunity must be given for a Defence and evidence to be filed.

(iv) DISCRETION OF THE COURT:

- The court has no discretion to separate the claim for possession from the claim for arrears / the counterclaim, since the one relies on the other absolutely (Baygreen Properties Limited v Gil, Court of Appeal (2002)).

- If the court considers that any counterclaim would amount to merely a fanciful defence of set off, then the court continues to be obliged to make a possession order under Ground 8 where pleaded and made out, and may make a possession order under Grounds 10 or 11 if reasonable to do so.

Baygreen Properties Limited v Gil, Court of Appeal (2002)

LORD JUSTICE CLARKE: "… where a tenant asserts an arguable breach of [the landlord's] obligations the court must investigate them and the rent "lawfully due" from the tenant is the rent after deduction of the amount of any equitable set off… I would so hold because the basis of an equitable set off is that it impeaches the title to the legal demand".

DEFENCE OF SET-OFF BY WAY OF A COUNTERCLAIM: DEPOSIT PROTECTION / SERVICE OF PRESCRIBED INFORMATION

1. **If a deposit was taken, was it protected and the prescribed information served by the relevant deadline?**

    (i) Was a deposit taken and protected within the prescribed period / and the prescribed information served within the prescribed period?

Deposit Protection and Service of Prescribed Information Deadlines for the Purposes of a Counterclaim

AST commenced	Deposit received by LL	(i) Deposit must be protected by, and (ii) service of prescribed information required by	Authority
Any time	On or after 6 April 2012	30 days of receipt of the deposit	Ss 213(3) and 213(6) Housing Act 2004
Any time	Between 6 April 2007 and 5 April 2012 inclusive	**Before** 6 May 2012	Art. 16 Localism Act 2011 (Commencement No. 4 and Transitional, Transitory and Saving Provisions) Order 2012
Before 6 April 2007 and becoming statutory periodic on or after 6 April 2007	Before 6 April 2007	**Before** 23 June 2015	s215A Housing Act 2004

Before 6 April 2007 and becoming statutory periodic before 6 April 2007	Before 6 April 2007	N/A – no counterclaim available	N/A – no counterclaim available

NOTE – Service of the prescribed information means the FULL prescribed information (see relevant section in relation to Section 21 notices). It is notable that if the LL is a company the certificate does NOT need to be signed in accordance with s44 Companies Act 2006 (Northwood (Solihull) Ltd v Fearne & Ors, Court of Appeal (2022)).

(ii) If not, then DEFENCE OF SET-OFF BY WAY OF A COUNTERCLAIM:

- A Section 214 claim may be brought in respect of the breach identified (s214(1) Housing Act 2004).
- This claim <u>must</u> be worth between 1 and 3 times the value of the deposit (s214(2) and (4) Housing Act 2004) (in addition to the return of the deposit (s214(3) Housing Act 2004)).
- Failure to the provide the prescribed information may be worth 3 times the value of the deposit even where the deposit was in fact protected (Ayannuga v Swindells, Court of Appeal (2012)).
- This provides a set-off to the arrears claimed.
- This EITHER contributes to a wider defence of set-off OR is sufficient of a Defence to this claim to defeat the claim / may defeat the claim.

(iii) DISCRETION OF THE COURT:

- If the court is satisfied as to the breach and is satisfied that a counterclaim may (3 times the deposit plus return of the deposit itself) defeat ground 8 (if relied upon) (in addition to any other counterclaims) then it has no discretion not to make directions for a Defence and Counterclaim to be filed. A defence of set off impugns the landlord's legal title to the arrears.

Section 213 Housing Act 2004

...

(6) The information required by subsection (5) must be given to the tenant and any relevant person—

(a) in the prescribed form or in a form substantially to the same effect, and

(b) within the period of 30 days beginning with the date on which the deposit is received by the landlord.

Section 214 Housing Act 2004

(1) Where a tenancy deposit has been paid in connection with a shorthold tenancy on or after 6 April 2007, the tenant or any relevant person... may make an application to the county court on the grounds—

(a) that section 213(3) or (6) has not been complied with in relation to the deposit, or

(b) that he has been notified by the landlord that a particular authorised scheme applies to the deposit but has been unable to obtain confirmation from the scheme administrator that the deposit is being held in accordance with the scheme.

(2) Subsections (3) and (4) apply in the case of an application under subsection (1) if the tenancy has not ended and the court—

(a) is satisfied that section 213(3) or (6) has not been complied with in relation to the deposit, or

(b) is not satisfied that the deposit is being held in accordance with an authorised scheme,

(3) The court must, as it thinks fit, either—

(a) order the person who appears to the court to be holding the deposit to repay it to the applicant, or

(b) order that person to pay the deposit into the designated account held by the scheme administrator under an authorised custodial scheme, within the period of 14 days beginning with the date of the making of the order.

(4) The court must order the landlord to pay to the applicant a sum of money not less than the amount of the deposit and not more than three times the amount of the deposit within the period of 14 days beginning with the date of the making of the order.

<u>Northwood (Solihull) Ltd v Cooke, Fearne & Ors, Court of Appeal (2022)</u>

LORD JUSTICE LEWISON: "The [trial] judge took the view that whether or not the certificate had been signed by the landlord was "a binary matter". Either it had or it had not, and if it had not, then the certificate could not be saved by saying that it was substantially to the same effect. The first flaw in this reasoning, in my judgment, is once again that it proceeds on the assumption that only "execution by" the landlord in accordance with section 44 of the Companies Act is permitted. But as we have seen, section 212(9) expressly extends the definition of landlord so as to include a person acting on behalf of the landlord... In this case, the certificate gave the tenants all the information it was required to do, and was signed by a person authorised (both by the landlord and by Section 212(9)) to sign it. It fulfilled all the statutory purposes it was required to fulfil. I would hold that it was substantially to the like effect, and hence was valid".

<u>Ayannuga v Swindells, Court of Appeal (2012)</u>

LORD JUSTICE ETHERTON: "I would vary the Deputy District Judge's order [by ordering] that the Respondent do repay the deposit... and also do pay... three times the amount of the deposit".

<u>FOR OTHER AUTHORITIES SEE THE EARLIER SECTION ON DEPOSIT PROTECTION AND SECTION 21 NOTICES.</u>

DEFENCE OF SET-OFF BY WAY OF A COUNTERCLAIM: BREACHES OF THE EQUALITY ACT (DISCRIMINATION AND HARASSMENT)

1. **Has the LL (or the LL's agent) discriminated against the Defendant's protected characteristic or harassed the Defendant?**

   (i) Does the Defendant possess a protected characteristic, has the LL (or his agent) discriminated against the Defendant as a result of this protected characteristic, AND has this caused the Defendant injury to feelings?

   - The protected characteristics (as they apply to property management):
     - disability;
     - gender reassignment;
     - pregnancy and maternity;
     - race;
     - religion or belief;
     - sex;
     - sexual orientation

   (ii) If yes, then DEFENCE OF SET-OFF BY WAY OF A COUNTERCLAIM FOR DISCRIMINATION:

   - It is unlawful for a landlord (or agent) to discriminate, harass, or victimise the Defendant on account of the Defendant's protected characteristic, in respect of the way in which the landlord lets the property or in respect of any other property management decision or in any other way (ss 33-35 Equality Act 2010).

- The county court has the jurisdiction to impose sanctions for such breaches of equality legislation (ss 114-115 Equality Act 2010).

- The remedies available, in terms of valuing the potential counterclaim, will include compensation for injured feelings (s119(4) Equality Act 2010).

- Some relevant factors in evidencing any such counterclaim will include:

How serious was the discrimination?	What was said or done? How was it said or done? Was it said or done in private or in public?
Testimony of the Defendant / Part 20 Claimant	How did the discrimination make the Defendant feel, and for how long? Did it stop them from doing things that they otherwise would have done? Were they upset by specifics, or by the general situation? There need to be directions for witness statements.
Any medical evidence available?	Did the Defendant develop symptoms as a result of the discrimination (such as depression) which required medical intervention?

- Compensation is typically awarded in line with the Vento scale (three bandings, from minor to severe). The Vento scale band values are updated annually in March or April. The current banding values, from 6 April 2022, are as follows:

<table>
<tr><th>LOWER BAND</th><th>MIDDLE BAND</th><th>UPPER BAND</th></tr>
<tr><td>£990 – £9,900</td><td>£9,900 – £29,600</td><td>£29,600 -£49,300</td></tr>
<tr><td rowspan="2">Less serious cases, e.g. a one-off or isolated incident</td><td>Serious cases which do not fall into the upper band</td><td>Most serious cases, e.g. a sustained campaign of harassment or discrimination</td></tr>
<tr><td colspan="2">E.g. Particularly rude language / public not private / the discrimination relates to an intimate area of the Defendant's life, such as sexual or medical / the Defendant becomes ill or depressed as a result of the incident(s).</td></tr>
</table>

SOURCE: Vento v Chief Constable of West Yorkshire Police, Court of Appeal (2002), and the Fifth Addendum to Presidential Guidance (updating the Vento Bands), 28 March 2022.

- The Defendant's claim has a value which [even in less serious cases may amount to up to £9,900]. This would amount to a defence of set off against the arrears.

- This EITHER contributes to a wider defence of set-off OR is sufficient of a Defence to this claim to defeat the claim / may defeat the claim.

- The case should be adjourned and directions given for a Defence [and witness statements, or adjourned for a directions hearing].

(iii) DISCRETION OF THE COURT:

- If the claim is disputed on grounds which appear to be substantial, then the court has no discretion but to adjourn and give directions for a Defence.

NOTE: Personal injury valuations also make use of the Vento scale.

MORE BOOKS BY LAW BRIEF PUBLISHING

A selection of our other titles available now:-

'A Practical Guide to Parental Alienation in Private and Public Law Children Cases' by Sam King QC & Frankie Shama
'Contested Heritage – Removing Art from Land and Historic Buildings' by Richard Harwood QC, Catherine Dobson, David Sawtell
'The Limits of Separate Legal Personality: When Those Running a Company Can Be Held Personally Liable for Losses Caused to Third Parties Outside of the Company' by Dr Mike Wilkinson
'A Practical Guide to Transgender Law' by Robin Moira White & Nicola Newbegin
'Artificial Intelligence – The Practical Legal Issues (2nd Edition)' by John Buyers
'A Practical Guide to Residential Freehold Conveyancing' by Lorraine Richardson
'A Practical Guide to Pensions on Divorce for Lawyers' by Bryan Scant
'A Practical Guide to Challenging Sham Marriage Allegations in Immigration Law' by Priya Solanki
'A Practical Guide to Legal Rights in Scotland' by Sarah-Jane Macdonald
'A Practical Guide to New Build Conveyancing' by Paul Sams & Rebecca East
'A Practical Guide to Defending Barristers in Disciplinary Cases' by Marc Beaumont
'A Practical Guide to Inherited Wealth on Divorce' by Hayley Trim
'A Practical Guide to Practice Direction 12J and Domestic Abuse in Private Law Children Proceedings' by Rebecca Cross & Malvika Jaganmohan
'A Practical Guide to Confiscation and Restraint' by Narita Bahra QC, John Carl Townsend, David Winch
'A Practical Guide to the Law of Forests in Scotland' by Philip Buchan
'A Practical Guide to Health and Medical Cases in Immigration Law' by Rebecca Chapman & Miranda Butler
'A Practical Guide to Bad Character Evidence for Criminal Practitioners by Aparna Rao
'A Practical Guide to Extradition Law post-Brexit' by Myles Grandison et al

'A Practical Guide to Hoarding and Mental Health for Housing Lawyers' by Rachel Coyle
'A Practical Guide to Psychiatric Claims in Personal Injury – 2nd Edition' by Liam Ryan
'Stephens on Contractual Indemnities' by Richard Stephens
'A Practical Guide to the EU Succession Regulation' by Richard Frimston
'A Practical Guide to Solicitor and Client Costs – 2nd Edition' by Robin Dunne
'Constructive Dismissal – Practice Pointers and Principles' by Benjimin Burgher
'A Practical Guide to Religion and Belief Discrimination Claims in the Workplace' by Kashif Ali
'A Practical Guide to the Law of Medical Treatment Decisions' by Ben Troke
'Fundamental Dishonesty and QOCS in Personal Injury Proceedings: Law and Practice' by Jake Rowley
'A Practical Guide to the Law in Relation to School Exclusions' by Charlotte Hadfield & Alice de Coverley
'A Practical Guide to Divorce for the Silver Separators' by Karin Walker
'The Right to be Forgotten – The Law and Practical Issues' by Melissa Stock
'A Practical Guide to Planning Law and Rights of Way in National Parks, the Broads and AONBs' by James Maurici QC, James Neill et al
'A Practical Guide to Election Law' by Tom Tabori
'A Practical Guide to the Law in Relation to Surrogacy' by Andrew Powell
'A Practical Guide to Claims Arising from Fatal Accidents – 2nd Edition' by James Patience
'A Practical Guide to the Ownership of Employee Inventions – From Entitlement to Compensation' by James Tumbridge & Ashley Roughton
'A Practical Guide to Asbestos Claims' by Jonathan Owen & Gareth McAloon
'A Practical Guide to Stamp Duty Land Tax in England and Northern Ireland' by Suzanne O'Hara
'A Practical Guide to the Law of Farming Partnerships' by Philip Whitcomb
'Covid-19, Homeworking and the Law – The Essential Guide to Employment and GDPR Issues' by Forbes Solicitors
'Covid-19 and Criminal Law – The Essential Guide' by Ramya Nagesh
'Covid-19 and Family Law in England and Wales – The Essential Guide' by Safda Mahmood

'A Practical Guide to the Law of Unlawful Eviction and Harassment – 2nd Edition' by Stephanie Lovegrove

'Covid-19, Brexit and the Law of Commercial Leases – The Essential Guide' by Mark Shelton

'A Practical Guide to Costs in Personal Injury Claims – 2nd Edition' by Matthew Hoe

'A Practical Guide to the General Data Protection Regulation (GDPR) – 2nd Edition' by Keith Markham

'Ellis on Credit Hire – Sixth Edition' by Aidan Ellis & Tim Kevan

'A Practical Guide to Working with Litigants in Person and McKenzie Friends in Family Cases' by Stuart Barlow

'Protecting Unregistered Brands: A Practical Guide to the Law of Passing Off' by Lorna Brazell

'A Practical Guide to Secondary Liability and Joint Enterprise Post-Jogee' by Joanne Cecil & James Mehigan

'A Practical Guide to the Pre-Action RTA Claims Protocol for Personal Injury Lawyers' by Antonia Ford

'A Practical Guide to Neighbour Disputes and the Law' by Alexander Walsh

'A Practical Guide to Forfeiture of Leases' by Mark Shelton

'A Practical Guide to Coercive Control for Legal Practitioners and Victims' by Rachel Horman

'A Practical Guide to Rights Over Airspace and Subsoil' by Daniel Gatty

'Tackling Disclosure in the Criminal Courts – A Practitioner's Guide' by Narita Bahra QC & Don Ramble

'A Practical Guide to the Law of Driverless Cars – Second Edition' by Alex Glassbrook, Emma Northey & Scarlett Milligan

'A Practical Guide to TOLATA Claims' by Greg Williams

'A Practical Guide to Elderly Law – 2nd Edition' by Justin Patten

'A Practical Guide to Responding to Housing Disrepair and Unfitness Claims' by Iain Wightwick

'A Practical Guide to the Construction and Rectification of Wills and Trust Instruments' by Edward Hewitt

'A Practical Guide to the Law of Bullying and Harassment in the Workplace' by Philip Hyland

'How to Be a Freelance Solicitor: A Practical Guide to the SRA-Regulated Freelance Solicitor Model' by Paul Bennett

‘A Practical Guide to Prison Injury Claims’ by Malcolm Johnson
‘A Practical Guide to the Small Claims Track - 2nd Edition’ by Dominic Bright
‘A Practical Guide to Advising Clients at the Police Station’ by Colin Stephen McKeown-Beaumont
‘A Practical Guide to Antisocial Behaviour Injunctions’ by Iain Wightwick
‘Practical Mediation: A Guide for Mediators, Advocates, Advisers, Lawyers, and Students in Civil, Commercial, Business, Property, Workplace, and Employment Cases’ by Jonathan Dingle with John Sephton
‘The Mini-Pupillage Workbook’ by David Boyle
‘A Practical Guide to Crofting Law’ by Brian Inkster
‘A Practical Guide to Spousal Maintenance’ by Liz Cowell
‘A Practical Guide to the Law of Domain Names and Cybersquatting’ by Andrew Clemson
‘A Practical Guide to the Law of Gender Pay Gap Reporting’ by Harini Iyengar
‘A Practical Guide to the Rights of Grandparents in Children Proceedings’ by Stuart Barlow
‘NHS Whistleblowing and the Law’ by Joseph England
‘Employment Law and the Gig Economy’ by Nigel Mackay & Annie Powell
‘A Practical Guide to Noise Induced Hearing Loss (NIHL) Claims’ by Andrew Mckie, Ian Skeate, Gareth McAloon
‘An Introduction to Beauty Negligence Claims – A Practical Guide for the Personal Injury Practitioner’ by Greg Almond
‘Intercompany Agreements for Transfer Pricing Compliance’ by Paul Sutton
‘Zen and the Art of Mediation’ by Martin Plowman
‘A Practical Guide to the SRA Principles, Individual and Law Firm Codes of Conduct 2019 – What Every Law Firm Needs to Know’ by Paul Bennett
‘A Practical Guide to Adoption for Family Lawyers’ by Graham Pegg
‘A Practical Guide to Industrial Disease Claims’ by Andrew Mckie & Ian Skeate
‘A Practical Guide to Redundancy’ by Philip Hyland
‘A Practical Guide to Vicarious Liability’ by Mariel Irvine
‘A Practical Guide to Applications for Landlord’s Consent and Variation of Leases’ by Mark Shelton
‘A Practical Guide to Relief from Sanctions Post-Mitchell and Denton’ by Peter Causton

www.ingramcontent.com/pod-product-compliance
Lightning Source LLC
LaVergne TN
LVHW052309200926
848481LV00002B/507

* 9 7 8 1 9 1 4 6 0 8 4 9 0 *